Helion & Company Limited
Unit 8 Amherst Business Centre
Budbrooke Road
Warwick
CV34 5WE
England
Tel. 01926 499 619
Email: info@helion.co.uk
Website: www.helion.co.uk
Twitter: @helionbooks
Visit our blog https://helionbooks.wordpress.com/

Typeset by Oliver Barstow, Milan, Italy
Cover design by Paul Hewitt, Battlefield Design (www.battlefield-design.co.uk)

ISBN 978-1-804517-88-8

British Library Cataloguing-in-Publication Data
A catalogue record for this book is available from the British Library

We always welcome receiving book proposals from prospective authors.

Cover artwork:
Two T-6D Texans of 1° EMRA conduct a strike against the guerrillas in the Araguaia area, in the south-eastern Federal State of Pará, in May 1974. (Artwork by Renato Dalmaso)

CONTENTS

Note: In order to simplify the use of this book, all names, locations and geographic designations are as provided in *The Times World Atlas*, or other traditionally accepted major sources of reference, as of the time of described events.

ABBREVIATIONS AND ACRONYMS

AFB Air Force Base
ALADA *1ª Asa de Defesa Aérea* (1st Air Defence Wing) (FAB)
ARENA *Aliança Renovadora Nacional* (National Renewal Alliance)
BIS *Batalhão de Infantaria de Selva* (Jungle Infantry Battalion) (Brazilian Army)
CECAN *Centro do Corréio Aéreo Nacional* (National Air Mail Centre) (FAB)
CATRE *Centro de Aplicações Táticas e Recomplementamento de Equipagens* (Tactical Applications and Equipment Replenishment Centre) (FAB)
CCC *Comando de Caça aos Comunistas* (Command for Hunting Communists)
CENIMAR *Centro de Informações da Marinha* (Navy Information Centre)
CFN *Corpo de Fuzileiros Navais* (Marine Corps) (Brazilian Navy)
CFPM *Centro de Formação de Pilotos Militares* (Military Pilot Training Centre) (FAB)
CIA Central Intelligence Agency (US)
CIEH *Centro de Instrução e Emprego de Helicópteros* (Helicopter Training and Utilisation Centre) (FAB)
CIEX *Centro de Inteligência do Exército* (Army Intelligence Centre)
CNBB *Conferência Nacional dos Bispos do Brasil* (National Conference of Bishops of Brazil)
DF *Distrito Federal* (Federal District)
DOI-CODI *Destacamento de Operações Internas-Comando Operacional de Defesa Interna* (Detachment of Internal Operations-Operational Command of Internal Defence)
DOPS *Departamento Estadual de Ordem Política e Social* (State Department of Political and Social Order) (Federal Police)
EB *Exército Brasileiro* (Brazilian Army)
ECA *Esquadrão de Comunicações e Alerta* (Communications and Alert Squadron) (FAB)
EDA *Esquadrão de Demonstração Aérea* (Air Demonstration Squadron) (FAB)
EIA *Esquadrão de Instrução Aérea* (Air Instruction Squadron) (FAB)
ELO *Esquadrilha de Ligação e Observação* (Liaison and Observation Squadron) (FAB)
EMBRAER *Empresa Brasileira de Aeronáutica S.A.* (Brazilian Aeronautics Company, Inc.)
EMRA *Esquadrão Misto de Reconhecimento e Ataque* (Reconnaissance and Attack Mixed Squadron) (FAB)
ERA *Esquadrão de Reconhecimento e Ataque* (Reconnaissance and Attack Squadron) (FAB)
ETA *Esquadrão de Transporte Aéreo* (Air Transport Squadron) (FAB)
FAB *Força Aérea Brasileira* (Brazilian Air Force)
FOGUERA *Força de Guerilha do Araguaia* (Araguaia Guerrilla Force)
GAE *Grupo de Aviação Embarcada* (Embarked Air Group) (FAB)
GAV *Grupo de Aviação* (Aviation Group) (FAB)
GAvCA *Grupo de Aviação de Caça* (Air Fighter Group) (FAB)
GDA *Grupo de Defesa Aérea* (Air Defence Group) (FAB)
GDP Gross Domestic Product
Gr11 *Grupos dos Onze* (Groups of Eleven)
GTA Araguaia Working Group
GT *Grupo de Transporte* (Transport Group) (FAB)
GTE *Grupo de Transporte Especial* (Special Transport Group) (FAB)
GTT *Grupo de Transporte de Tropas* (Troop Transport Group) (FAB)
LCU Landing Craft Utility
LCVP Landing Craft, Vehicle, Personnel (Higgins Boat)
MAC Anti-Communist Movement
MB *Marinha do Brasil* (Brazilian Navy)
MDB *Movimento Democrático Brasileiro* (Brazilian Democratic Movement)
MR-8 *Movimento Revolucionário 8 de Outubro* (8 October Revolutionary Movement)
MRMN *Movimento de Resistência Militar Nacionalista* (Nationalist Military Resistance Movement)
MRT *Movimento Revolucionário Tiradentes* (Tiradentes Revolutionary Movement)
OBAN *Operação Bandeirantes* (Operation Bandeirantes)
PCB *Partido Comunista Brasileiro* (Brazilian Communist Party)
PCBR *Partido Comunista Brasileiro Revolucionário* (Brazilian Revolutionary Communist Party)
PCdoB *Partido Comunista do Brasil* (Communist Party of Brazil)
PCR *Partido Comunista Revolucionário* (Revolutionary Communist Party)
PDS *Partido Democrático Social* (Social Democratic Party)
PF *Polícia Federal* (Federal Police)
PIC *Pelotão de Investigações Criminais* (Criminal Investigation Platoon) (Army)
PM *Polícia Militar* (Military Police)
PMDB *Partido do Movimento Democrático Brasileiro* (Brazilian Democratic Movement Party)
POLOP *Organização Revolucionária Marxista Política Operária* (Marxist Revolutionary Workers Political Organisation)
PRT *Partido Revolucionário dos Trabalhadores* (Workers' Revolutionary Party)
PT *Partido dos Trabalhadores* (Workers' Party)
PTB *Partido Trabalhista Brasileiro* (Brazilian Labour Party)

RAN	*Resistência Armada Nacionalista* (Nationalist Armed Resistance)
SNI	*Serviço Nacional de Informações* (National Information Service)
UNE	*União Nacional dos Estudantes* (National Union of Students)
VAR-Palmares	*Vanguarda Armada Revolucionaria-Palmares* (Revolutionary Armed Vanguard-Palmares)
VPR	*Vanguarda Popular Revolucionária* (Popular Revolutionary Vanguard)

ACKNOWLEDGEMENTS

The author wishes to express his deep gratitude to fellow Brazilian historian Hélio Higuchi for his invaluable help in the preparation of this volume, both with data and pictures. Without his help, this book would probably remain incomplete.

INTRODUCTION

In Volume 1, the military regimes that ruled Brazil during the 1960s, 1970s, and 1980s were examined. This included an overview of the various guerrilla groups operating within Brazil, as well as an analysis of the military strength of the Brazilian armed forces. This current volume focuses on the operational aspects of the conflict, detailing the guerrilla actions and the military operations that ultimately dismantled these groups. These efforts targeted not only the guerrillas in the Amazon region but also the urban factions. The military government's directive was explicitly to "wipe them off the map" at any cost, or, as they phrased it, to "root out the communist cancer"—a mission that was ruthlessly executed.

The final chapter of this volume analyzes the factors that led to the catastrophic failure of the guerrilla movements in Brazil, particularly those in the Amazon and their urban logistical support networks. Unlike Argentina, where top military leaders faced trials and convictions for alleged war crimes, Brazil saw no such accountability when its military relinquished power. As a result, the repression of guerrilla forces remains a taboo subject among Brazilian military circles, rarely discussed or investigated. Few have dared to publicly share their perspectives on this contentious history. This volume seeks to shed light on that dark and often-overlooked chapter in Brazil's past.

1
THE FIGHT AGAINST THE ARAGUAIA GUERRILLA

Background

In the 1960s, the region through which the Araguaia River runs was inhabited by Brazilians, mostly from other regions, mainly from the northeast of the country, but there were also aboriginal people in the area. The former were those in search of land for cultivation, miners seeking precious stones, hunters in search of animal skins and immigrants wanting all kinds of work and riches that these virgin areas could offer. Entire families, fleeing the northeastern drought in Brazil, worked on farms for less than a minimum wage. Many planted manioc and chestnut, and most of them were illiterate and exploited by the few landowners.[1] It was the ideal place, according to the PCdoB, for the start of a popular uprising. The same assessment, after the discovery of the guerrilla uprising, was made by the Navy Information Centre (*Centro de Informações da Marinha*, CENIMAR), which reported that the population of the region lived in misery, under the domination of major landowners and corrupt municipal authorities.

Eighteen PCdoB members started political-military guerrilla training in the People's Republic of China in 1964, as the Party adopted the line of prolonged people's war inspired by Mao Zedong. (Open source)

The preparations of the PCdoB guerrillas dated back to 1964, when the first militants began political and military training in the People's Republic of China, the party seeking to prolong the people's war inspired by Mao Zedong. This preference for an armed struggle was contrary to the idea of a Cuban 'focus' and the continental Marxist-Leninist revolution. Between 1964 and 1968, 18 Brazilian militants received military training in China, including several who were then settling in Araguaia. In Brazil, a first group of would-be guerrillas carried out their initial training in a house at São Vicente in Baixada Santista, under the direction and coordination of Armando Giménez – former director of the PCdoB in São Paulo – and Osvaldo Orlando da Costa.

Four months after the 1964 military coup, Brazilian Army officers and sergeants were sent for a jungle combat course in Panama, where

Various scenes from the city of Xambioá in the state of Goiás (present day Tocantins): the main avenue in the 1960s and a typical dirt street of the city (above). Xambioá in the 1970s, with the Araguaia River in the background and an FAB DHC-5 Buffalo on the city's runway around 1972 (below). (Open source)

The city of Marabá, in the state of Pará, on the Tocantins River, which was the main base of the Army during operations in Araguaia between 1972 and 1974. Below, the Marabá Aerodrome, still with an unpaved runway, with a VARIG Douglas DC-3. (Open source)

An aerial view of the dense Amazon jungle, watered by mighty rivers. These characteristics made it the ideal place for a guerrilla rising, due to difficult access and the inability of the military to carry out good aerial reconnaissance. (Open source)

The first seven guerrillas who moved to the area known as the Parrot's Beak from Maranhão in 1967. (Open source)

they were taught at a training centre run by the US Army. At that time, the Brazilian armed forces began a study into carrying out anti-guerrilla operations, being involved in secret planning that lasted about two years. The military was seeking to prevent the launching of similar insurgent movements in other regions of Brazil, fearing that an outbreak of violence in rural regions could destabilise military power in the country. Between 1969 and 1971, the military dismantled infiltration attempts and small bases of the ALN and VAR-Palmares organisations in the Bico do Papagaio region without major difficulties, in what was known as Operation Mesopotamia, which included troop manoeuvres carried out around Imperatriz in Maranhão. However, the source of the PCdoB guerrillas, in the area around Araguaia, Xambioá and Marabá, remained unknown.

The region could be used to hide political opponents wanted by the military regimes in all urban areas of Brazil. It was also remote enough to allow the guerrillas time to put down roots. Their plan was to establish dwellings like those of the peasants and then start winning their confidence by giving basic lessons in health and farming. During this phase of their plan, the subversives would not reveal their real intentions.

The first combatants began to arrive in the area in 1967, coming from the south, southeast and Maranhão, where they had already settled. Among them were João Amazonas, the main leader of the party, Elza Monnerat, Maurício Grabois, his son André Grabois, his son-in-law Gilberto Olímpio Maria, Doctor João Carlos Haas Sobrinho and the giant black engineer and boxing champion Osvaldo Orlando da Costa (known as *Osvaldão*).

Between 1967 and 1971, the insurgents settled in as local inhabitants and became a part of the area's humble society, opening small shops and bars, providing minor medical services from house to house, delivering babies, hunting, fishing, planting, transporting people and food in canoes, opening a pharmacy, giving classes to residents and carrying out political propaganda in small-scale meetings. They were known as *Paulistas* by the local mixed race *caboclos*.[2] From the first dozen that had arrived in 1967–1968, by the beginning of the 1970s the group had more than 60 militants, men and women from different parts of Brazil, almost all of them young university students or liberal professionals, preparing for a revolution which they believed would begin there. Using *noms de guerre*, they were known as *Cid*, *Mário*, *Dr Juca*, *Dona Maria*, *Dina*, *Baianinha*, *Regina*, *Sônia*, *Zeca Fogoió*, *Mariadina* and *Cazuza* among others, by the residents of Araguaia. They included former students of chemistry, architecture, geography, engineering, literature, physics, astronomy, medicine, geology and teaching, and there was even a trio of brothers, the Petit da Silvas.

The first phase of their plan ran smoothly, but by 1972 the military intelligence services had already uncovered the guerrilla attempt in the Araguaia area, and the first clashes were about to begin. On 12 April 1972, six years after the arrival of the first communist militants, direct confrontations with the state security forces started. By then, the guerrilla groups were scattered near the municipalities of Marabá, São Domingos do Araguaia, São Geraldo do Araguaia, São Sebastião, Araguatins, Tocantinópolis, Xambioá and Brejo Grande do Araguaia.

The Organisation of the Araguaia Guerrilla Force (*Força de Guerilha do Araguaia*, FOGUERA)

By May 1972, when military operations effectively began, FOGUERA had 85 guerrillas – of which around 15 were women – spread over an area of around 6,500km^2, which covered the main municipalities and villages in the southeastern state of Pará. FOGUERA was the armed wing of the People's Liberation Movement (*Movimento de Libertação do Povo*, MLP).

The MLP was organised into a Political Bureau, a Military Commission, three detachments, each with three groups of between eight and 10 guerrillas, and combat groups. The Political Bureau was the top body of the PCdoB, at that time a dissident group from the PCB that followed Soviet guidance, while the PCdoB followed the Chinese line. Adopting the principles advocated by Mao Zedong, the PCdoB idealised the outbreak of a guerrilla movement in rural areas that, after receiving support from the local population, would be extended to urban centres. The members of the Political Bureau were rarely in the area, but they guided and closely monitored everything that was going on there. All decisions of the Military Commission were subject to approval by the Political Bureau. The leadership of the party in São Paulo was initially composed of João Amazonas (known as *Cid* or *Velho Cid*), Maurício Grabois (known as *Mario*) and Ángelo Arroyo (known as *Joaquim*). They were later joined by Dr João Carlos Haas Sobrinho (known as *Juca*) and Gilberto Olímpio Maria.

The Military Commission constituted the operation command of FOGUERA. Its duties were to plan, coordinate and conduct the actions of the guerrilla force. This leadership, as well as the other elements in command roles in the detachments and groups, was almost entirely made up of cadres who had taken guerrilla courses abroad, notably in Beijing, Tirana and Havana. It was initially composed of João

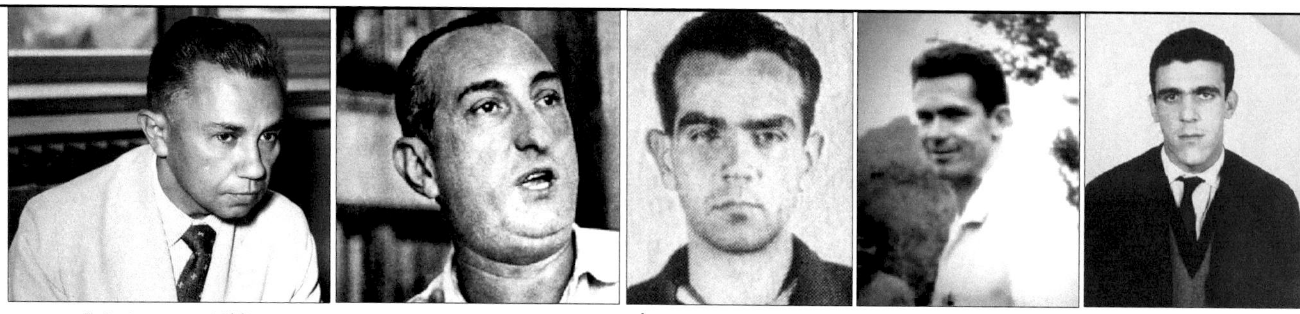

João Amazonas (*Cid*) Maurício Grabois (*Mario*) Ángelo Arroyo (*Joaquim*) João Carlos Haas (*Juca*) Gilberto Olimpio María (*Pedro*)

Members of the Political Bureau of the PCdoB, the top leadership of FOGUERA. (Open source)

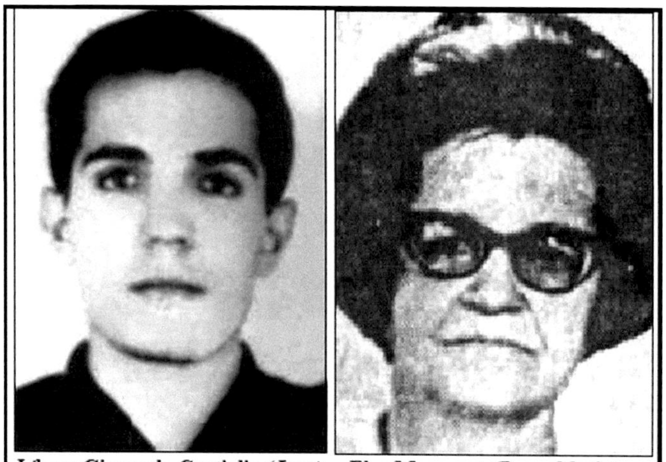

Líbero Giancarlo Castiglia (*Joca*) Elza Monnerat (*Dona María*)

Besides all the members of the Political Bureau, who were also in the Military Commission, two other guerrillas were in the FOGUERA Military Commission. (Open source)

Amazonas, Maurício Grabois, Elza Monerat, Ángelo Arroyo, João Carlos Haas, Gilberto Olímpio Maria and Líbero Giancarlo Castiglia.

Three detachments were subordinated to the Military Commission, the operational elements of FOGUERA:

> Detachment A Faveiro, in the north, operated along the Transamazônica highway, in the regions of Faveiro, Fazenda São José, São João do Araguaia and Metade. The commander was André Grabois (known as *Zé Carlos*) and the vice commander Antônio de Pádua Costa (known as *Piauí*).
>
> Detachment B Gameleira, in the centre, covered the northeast of the Serra das Andorinhas, in the Gameleira River valley. Its commander was Osvaldo Orlando da Costa (known as *Osvaldão*) and the vice commander José Huberto Bronca (known as *Zeca*).
>
> Detachment C Caiano, in the south, was located southwest of the Serra das Andorinhas, covering the bases of Pau Preto, Abóbora and Esperancinha. Its commander was Paulo Mendes Rodrigues (known as *Paulo*) and the vice commander José Toledo de Oliveira (known as *Vítor*).

They used constant movement through the forests and did not remain tied to their local bases. For reasons of security, these detachments operated in a compartmentalised manner, not being aware of the actions planned and conducted by the others. The deputy commander of the detachment acted as a political commissioner, committing himself to raising the political level and ideological awareness. The Military Commission's command and control system over detachments was based on 'point coverage', with a predetermined location, date and time, and established in an absolutely compartmentalised manner, again in order to ensure the maintenance of secrecy.

A total of nine Combat Groups were subordinated to the detachments, and these constituted the basic elements of the guerrilla force. Their autonomy was extremely restricted and they operated under strict control of the detachment commanders.

For the most part, the elements belonging to FOGUERA were recruited by the PCdoB from university circles in the major urban centres of Fortaleza, Salvador, Rio de Janeiro and São Paulo. A good number were already living underground and committed to urban terrorism. Guerrilla training was carried out with the basic aim of achieving two objectives, one of a practical nature and the other theoretical. The practical part was aimed at preparing individual combatants and small groups for combat in a jungle environment, with guidance instructions, ambushes, and explosives and destruction with improvised materials. The theoretical part had the specific objective

André Grabois (Zé Carlos) Commander — Antônio de Padua Costa (Piauí) Vice Commander — DETACHMENT A - FAVEIRO

Osvaldo Orlando da Costa (Osvaldão) Commander — José Huberto Bronca (Zeca) Vice Commander — DETACHMENT B - GAMELEIRA

Paulo Mendes Rodriguez (Paulo) Commander — José Toledo de Oliveira (Vítor) Vice Commander — DETACHMENT C - CAIANO

Commanders and Vice Commanders of the three guerrilla detachments. (Open source)

One of the few guerrillas who survived, José Genoíno Netto (known as *Geraldo*). On the left, he is promoting communist ideas before peasants in the Araguaia area, and on the right, he is handcuffed after being captured by the Army. (Open source)

of strengthening the ideological awareness of FOGUERA members. It must be recognised that, in general, morale and belief in the cause were high. In addition to guerrilla training, the groups were also engaged in 'productive work', especially on farms, the main purpose being to create their own supplies.

The guerrillas developed psychological action with the local rural population known as 'mass work', with the aim of obtaining their support. This bore fruit in some areas with the organisation of a support force. But at no point was FOGUERA able to recruit elements of the local population who were willing to fight and effectively integrate with the guerrilla force. In fact, FOGUERA was still in its infancy as a guerrilla force. Their armament was limited to pistols and revolvers, hunting weapons and some rifles obtained from isolated actions against Military Police posts in Pará. One of the most serious mistakes made by the Federal armed forces was to start operations by triggering actions that were normally carried out against experienced and well-organised guerrilla forces who were ready for combat.

Despite their efforts to blend in with the locals, the insurgents' appearance, manners and way of expressing themselves did not match the older population already settled in Araguaia. While these 'knowledgeable people', mostly young, white, university educated youngsters, were accepted by the peasants, they did not deceive them. The local population called them *Paulistas*, as the guerrillas mainly came from large cities in the states of São Paulo and Minas Geráis. When one of the guerrillas told a local *caboclo* that one of *Cid*'s nephews was good with a machete, he received the answer, 'He must be really good with a pen', as he looked too intellectual to be fighting in the jungle (the machete being the traditional symbol of a Brazilian peasant working in agriculture, while the pen symbolised university students).

Little by little, the group grew, providing medical services for the local population and teaching literacy classes that gained the esteem of the people. With an average age of less than 30, at the height of their physical vigour, they stocked up on food, ammunition and medicine in scattered areas of the forests and underwent military training, getting used to life in the jungle. They learned how to make a fire and how to walk 200 meters through dense forest without getting lost. Constant training meant that some of them were able to survive alone in the forests, taking with them only weapons, ammunition, salt and flour.

On New Year's Eve in 1971, the different groups joined together in a celebration, imagining they would soon be able to launch their operations, confidence being high after their time training in the jungle. Prior to this, it was not a combat-ready guerrilla organisation. With few weapons and few members, the PCdoB leadership believed another year or two of preparation was needed before they could start the revolutionary rural guerrilla war that had been a political line of the party since 1962. However, an escape, a withdrawal and two arrests made in Fortaleza and São Paulo, far from Araguaia, would make the armed forces' intelligence services aware of the guerrillas earlier than expected and desired by the subversives.

Beginnings

The idea of establishing a rural guerrilla that could function as a centre to attract all the elements dissatisfied with the Brazilian military regime, compensating for the crushing of urban opposition movements, had been nurtured among leftist elements in Brazil since 1964. However, the PCdoB was the only political organisation that really tried to build such a focus.

The area selected by the PCdoB proved to be extremely suitable for subversive action. It was a region where the standard of living of the population was quite precarious; there was little presence of the state and municipal governments; the hospital and health networks were highly deficient; malaria and leishmaniasis were endemic, and a large part of the population was anaemic and infested with vermin. There was no treated water and much less a sewage system in the towns. The region's economy was based on the extraction of plants, with chestnut collection in the winter and wood cutting in the summer being the main activities. Agriculture was basically of a subsistence nature, with fields of corn, cassava and rice, and the population's quality of life was thus very low.

On the other hand, the position of the area, close to important road axes, was extremely favourable, and the region receiving a considerable number of new settlers which allowed reinforcements to arrive secretly. Militarily, the choice of location was a very intelligent one, the region encompassing the territory of two Military Area Commands, the Amazon and the Planalto, so there was no unity of command for Federal forces. At the beginning of operations, this caused coordination and control problems for government troops, constituting an advantage for the guerrilla force.

At the beginning of 1972, the government discovered the existence of the guerrillas and gathered information from various informants. In November 1971, two guerrillas – Pedro Albuquerque and his wife – had fled from the area, giving up on the subversive campaign. In January 1972, he was arrested in Fortaleza, Ceará, and the Army Intelligence Centre (*Centro de Inteligência do* Exército, CIEX) obtained information from him that led to the location of the guerrillas. Further information came from São Paulo. The wife of guerrilla Lúcio Petit da Silva (one of the Petit brothers) contracted hepatitis and tuberculosis in the jungle. She left Araguaia at the end of 1971 while pregnant and with problems caused by a poorly performed medical procedure,

The first two commanders of the Army troops in Araguaia: Major Generals Hugo Abreu (left) and Olavo Viana Moog (right). (*Exército Brasileiro*)

Army troops mobilised for the Araguaia area had to travel hundreds of kilometres in convoys of trucks and other military vehicles. (*Exército Brasileiro*)

being taken to Goiânia for treatment. She was supposed to return to the insurgents, but she fled the hospital and went to São Paulo to the home of her family, revealing information about her former comrades in return for being kept alive and out of prison.

Combining the information received, cross-referencing data and mapping the region, the government located the area being used by the guerrillas and estimated their strength. In March 1972, Federal Police agents visited Xambioá and asked about outsiders. As there were other small pockets of subversives scattered throughout the Amazon, the guerrillas, despite being warned, thought these moves did not concern them. On 12 April, under the command of Major General Olavo Viana Moog and paratrooper commander Major General Hugo Abreu, Brazilian Army troops entered Araguaia, in the area between Marabá and Xambioá. In each of those cities, a battalion of 400 men was deployed, while in the jungle, six combat bases were installed, each with a company, and by August of that year there were already 1,500 men deployed. The soldiers were armed with FAL assault rifles, while the NCOs and officers had submachine guns and pistols. Their firepower was far superior to that of the guerrillas, who were poorly armed and had unreliable weapons. As far as the general population and the press were concerned, these Army troops were simply participating in a training manoeuvre. A command post was established near Marabá, in a ravine on the bank of the Itacaiúnas River. The guerrillas, who had intended to surprise the military regime, were in their turn surprised by the vast military deployment in the Araguaia area.

Starting in 1972, when several of its members had already been established in the region for at least six years, the guerrillas were hit hard by the Brazilian Army. Combat operations were carried out on the border of the states of Goiás, Pará and Maranhão. The name of the subversives' movement came from the fact that its fighters settled on the banks of the Araguaia River, near the cities of São Geraldo, Pará and Xambioá, in the north of Goiás, currently located in the north of Tocantins, a region popularly known as Bico do Papagaio. The region had been chosen by the insurgents because it was the location of tensions between local farmers and developers, mainly miners and public works contractors who were attracted by the investment opportunities offered by the recent opening of the nearby Carajás iron ore mine. The guerrillas hoped to benefit from such tensions by siding with the peasants.

It is estimated that the movement was made up of about 85 guerrillas. Of these, only 17 would survive, among them José Genoíno, later president of the Workers' Party, who was detained by the Army in 1972 during the first stage of military operations. The vast majority of the combatants, composed mainly of former university students and self-employed workers, died in battle in the jungle or were executed after being arrested and tortured during the final stages of military operations in 1973 and 1974. However, none of these people were officially recognised as being dead, instead remaining in the category of 'missing persons' for political reasons. Currently, 60 of the combatants are still considered as 'missing'.

The Military Operations

Prior to the armed actions against the guerrilla, the Army formed the Jungle Infantry Battalion in Marabá in January 1970, and in October of that year the zone was declared a National Security Area.

Army troops initially arrived in the cities of Marabá and Xambioá and then settled in six camps in the jungle. (*Exército Brasileiro*)

A FAB Grumman SA-16A Albatross. (FAB)

Operação Carajás 70 (Operation Carajás 70)

On a sunny Amazonian morning in November 1970, a FAB Grumman SA-16 Albatross aircraft transported 12 special forces detachment paratroopers of the Airborne Brigade for a military exercise in the area of the Tocantins River, near the town of Marabá in the state of Pará. The paratroopers jumped from 7,000ft in a bold operation, considering the small size of the drop area, a small sandbank in the middle of the river. After a delay of 30 seconds, they opened their parachutes and the team leader released a Brazilian flag from his equipment. The team landed safely and quickly took the flag to a Navy vessel, where a Marine Corps lieutenant received it from the paratroopers. The river patrol ship moved from the island to the city port, where the marine officer, in a solemn manner, disembarked and passed the flag to a lieutenant from one of the Jungle Infantry Battalions of the Amazon Military Command (CMA). Duly escorted by an honour guard, the jungle infantryman headed to the city's main square, where he passed the flag to a public school student who, to the sound of the national anthem, proceeded to raise the national flag. This ceremony, one of great civic significance that was attended by thousands of inhabitants of the progressive city, marked the end of what had been the first major military operation carried out by the Brazilian armed forces in the Amazon region, known as Operation Carajás 70.[3]

The government's first suspicion of the presence of communist subversives came in 1970. However, they had no idea of the extent of the enemy forces, so in such circumstances they carried out a major military exercise in the region of Marabá. Operation Carajás 70 was a classic military exercise for a hypothetical confrontation between two rival armies (Blue versus Red), with the deployment of a large contingent of troops including the dropping of paratroopers and bombs on simulated targets. Several FAB aircraft participated in the exercise, including Douglas C-47 Skytrains, De Havilland Canada DHC-5 Buffalos and Beech D-18 transport units, Bell UH-1D/H

FAB Douglas C-47 serial 2009 flying over the Amazon River area. (Courtesy Albert Grandolini)

FAB De Havilland Canada DHC-5 Buffalo serial 2350. (Courtesy Albert Grandolini)

Bell UH-1D/H helicopters and Cessna O-1 Bird Dog aircraft were widely used by the FAB in the Amazon area in the fight against the guerrilla. (Courtesy Albert Grandolini, Helio Higuchi)

Iroquois helicopters, Cessna L-19 Bird Dog observation aircraft and North American T-6D Texan armed reconnaissance aircraft, which were based in several cities, particularly in Marabá and Imperatriz.

Employing personnel from the three armed forces, and with the participation of several units not based in the Amazon, Operation Carajás 70 simulated a counterinsurgency situation in a jungle environment and constituted excellent joint training for those taking part. However, more than a training exercise, the operation had as its main objective a demonstration of presence and deterrence, considering that, at that time, signs had become increasingly obvious of the presence of a rural guerrilla 'focus' in the region known as the Bico do Papagaio (Parrot's Beak), on the border of the states of Maranhão, Pará and Goiás.

The military exercise, despite being successful, did not bring consistent information about the presence of an enemy force, a fact that was only confirmed later. Indeed, around 18 months later, in April 1972, intelligence agencies confirmed the existence of insurgents in the regions of Marabá and Xambioá. The then-illegal PCdoB, with its Maoist orientation, had installed a training area there with a view to the subsequent development of a liberated zone.

The Araguaia Guerrilla Force, as the revolutionary movement called itself, was supported by a large amount of resources provided by the international communist movement, the majority of which came from Albania. The commitment of the Communist Party of Albania to FOGUERA was such that every day, at 9:00 p.m. local Xambioá time, an hour-long shortwave radio program, in Portuguese, was aired by a station in Tirana, the capital of Albania. The program was specifically aimed at the Araguaia movement, with the most recent events that occurred in the area being broadcast, always giving a heroic connotation to the guerrilla's actions. There was a long-range radio network integrating the guerrilla force, an intermediate station and Tirana. Dismantling this radio connection was one of the first challenges successfully overcome by Federal intelligence and security agencies.

The military intervention of the regime to eliminate the Araguaia Guerrilla was carried out through several operations, as described below.

Operação Mesopotâmia (Operation Mesopotamia)

This operation was launched by the Brazilian Army between 2 and 12 August 1971, and involved around 40 agents, including nine officers, belonging to the CIEX, Planalto Military Command, 11th Military Region and 3rd Infantry Brigade, under the command of Brigadier General Antônio Bandeira de Mello. Its objective was to

A FAB Douglas C-47 on a runway in the Amazon region, used to quickly transport troops to the Araguaia area in 1972. (FAB)

collect information and arrest militants on the border between the states of Pará, Maranhão and Goiás. During the operation, the agents followed clues that would lead to militants from the PRT, AP, ALN, VAR-Palmares and Ala Vermelha in that region.

Operation Mesopotamia provided excellent experience, in operational terms and military doctrine, for subsequent incursions in the Araguaia region. The agents travelled through the area to cities such as Imperatriz, Lagoa Verde, Porto Franco, Tocantinópolis, Araguatins, Trombas and Buritis. Dozens of activists and supporters (mostly peasants) were arrested. Air support from FAB aircraft was important to the operation, as well as Army troops who acted undercover disguised as civilians.

The objectives of this operation were three-fold: 1) dismantle the left-wing political movement in the area; 2) identify and arrest people considered subversive by the regime and identify other individuals in different locations across the country; 3) serve as a model for other operations.

Operações Peixe I, II, III, IV & V (Operations Fish I, II, III, IV & V)

These operations were executed between March and May 1972. Several incursions were carried out by military units commanded by the intelligence service with the aim of identifying and capturing infiltrated subversives. Very little was known about the size of the insurgent forces or their weapons. As they were reconnaissance missions, it was decided that those taking part would wear civilian clothes. Initially, no air support was dispatched. The only aerial element available was a Bell 205A1 helicopter (a civil version of the UH-1D), registration PT-HCR, belonging to *Companhia Meridional de Minação* (Southern Mining Company). This helicopter was used on loan in several transport and reconnaissance flights.

For Operation Fish I, the commander chosen was Lieutenant Nélio da Mata Rezende, from the 5th Company of Belém Guards, an elite unit of the Army Police. He led a group of seven agents in the Marabá region, all dressed as civilians and pretending to be ranchers looking for land to buy, but in reality they were on a covert mission to locate subversive training camps in the area, using data obtained from the subversive Pedro Albuquerque after his capture. This mission was entrusted to Lieutenant Rezende by Lieutenant Colonel Raúl Augusto Borges, Chief of the Second Section of the 8th Military Region. Once in the region, the agents toured certain areas by land and water, asking the farmers about the group of *Paulistas*, as the PCdoB subversives were locally known. They were immediately able to obtain data on the 'social action' activities carried out by the subversives, such as medical assistance. They swiftly managed to locate them 40km from Marabá and saw that they were armed with revolvers or pistols. The covert operation ended on 31 March, supplying a significant amount of data on the subversives in the area.

Once all the information gathered in Operation Fish I was processed, General Darcy Jardim de Mattos, Army Commander of the 8th Military Region, and Lieutenant Colonel Borges organised Operation Fish II. For this mission, 14 agents were chosen, divided into three groups, the first based in Marabá, which was to carry out the interrogations of the arrested suspects. This group was commanded by Frigate Captain Lima Barros of the Navy Information Centre and Lieutenant Rezende. The second team was to attack the Faveira area to capture four of the *Paulista* guerrillas and any other suspects. This team was led by NCOs Pinheiro and Cabral of the FAB and sergeants Morais and Bahía of the 5th Company of Army Guards. The third group was led by sergeants Lacy of the IV Naval District, Nascimento of the FAB First Air Zone and Hélio of the Army's 8th Military Region, who were to collect data and try to capture subversives in the area of the Trans-Amazonian Highway (*Rodovia Transamazônica*). To capture the guerrillas, they would have the support of a platoon from the 2nd Jungle Infantry Battalion and the Pará Military Police. All the agents in this operation were armed with assault rifles and submachine guns. They managed to capture several guerrillas and take them for interrogation, as well as stocks of weapons, ammunition and even a boat used for travelling on the rivers in the area.

On 12 April, Operation Fish III began, which was carried out by a platoon of the 2nd Jungle Infantry Battalion under Lieutenant Daiter Queiroz Maia. The platoon's 24 troops were transported to Marabá from Belém on a FAB Douglas C-47. They then advanced to the guerrilla camp located in an area called *Chega com Jeito* ('arrives with style'), but found it empty, the *Paulistas* having abandoned it two hours earlier. Weapons, ammunition, books on firearms and medicine, various documents and several other items abandoned by the guerrillas were seized.

During this period there were various clashes between guerrillas and government forces, with some guerrillas being captured, leading to the extraction of important information about the insurgent forces. The need to have helicopters to carry out missions soon became evident,

An Army exploration group in the Amazon jungle (left). A group of guerrillas in the jungle (right). (Open source)

A FAB Cessna L-19E Bird Dog (top) and a Bell UH-1H (bottom). (Hélio Higuchi/Col. Camazano)

and from May 1972 onwards, at least one FAB UH-1H helicopter and one Cessna L-19 plane were deployed to the region, along with more troops to fight the subversives.

There were suspicions that the guerrillas were receiving weapons from a communist country. The government did not know how they entered the country – whether by sea, land or air – so a plan was put into effect in order to patrol the Brazilian coast and some of the border areas. FAB Douglas B-26 attack aircraft, from the 1°/10° GAV (*Grupo de Aviação*) (1st Squadron of the 10th Aviation Group), based in Cumbica, São Paulo, were moved to Boa Vista in the state of Roraima, carrying out patrol and reconnaissance flights for several weeks. Likewise, FAB Lockheed P2V-5 Neptune aircraft, armed with 127mm SBAT rockets, from the 1°/7° GAV in Salvador, Bahía, patrolled the Brazilian coast throughout daylight hours in search of suspicious vessels.

Operation Fish IV was carried out in the area between Marabá and Xambioá. On 3 May 1972, a group of commanders met at the headquarters of the FAB's First Air Zone: colonels Rodopiano and Asis, Lieutenant Colonel Pinho and Captain Sirotenu of the FAB, the Commander of the IV Naval District, Lieutenant Colonel Borges of the Army and Colonel Douglas of the Pará Military Police. For Operation Fish IV, 10 troops were ordered to infiltrate the local population to obtain more information: from the Navy, NCO David and sergeants Lacy, Furtado and Lourine; from the FAB, sergeants Cabral and Nascimento; from the Army, Sergeant Morais, Corporal Rosa and Lieutenant Nélio Rezende, the latter being the commander of the mission; and from the Military Police, Colonel Douglas. They all worked undercover in civilian clothes. A doctor and three military nurses were added to the team for a supposed civic action mission among the population. The mission consisted of patrolling the Santa Cruz–Gameleira and Cocalinho–Couro D'Antas areas. The members of this mission were transported on a FAB C-47 to Xambioá. They then travelled aboard a civilian boat to Santa Cruz. With a civilian guide, they walked all the way to Couro D'Antas, asking local residents about the *Paulistas*. They located a guerrilla camp near the Gameleira River but found it empty. The next day, by chance, four members of the mission clashed with two guerrillas, one of whom was one of their detachment commanders, *Osvaldão*, and the other went by the

The Brazilian Air Force deployed Lockheed P2V-5 Neptune aircraft from the 1°/7° GAV armed with SBAT rockets (left) and Douglas B-26B Invaders from the 1°/10° GAV (right) to patrol the coast in search of suspicious vessels which could be bringing weapons to the Araguaia guerrillas. (Col. Camazano collection)

The guerrilla *Osvaldão* (left) killed the Army's Corporal Odílio Cruz Rosa (right) in the middle of the jungle. (Open source)

name *Simão*. In the subsequent confrontation, the Army suffered their first fatality in the fight against the guerrilla, Corporal Odílio Rosa, while Sergeant Morais was wounded. Following the clash, the surviving members of the mission dispersed and returned to Santa Cruz by separate paths. The first encounter with the guerrillas had been an abject failure for the Army.

On 9 May, Operation Fish V was mounted. This time, two platoons of the 2nd Jungle Infantry Battalion prepared to carry out the mission, in addition to a platoon from the 1st Jungle Infantry Battalion and a detachment of the Special Forces (paratroopers) led by Major Taumaturgo. The FAB carried out close support tasks with UH-1D helicopters and Cessna L-19 Bird Dogs. They entered the area where the first combat had occurred, managing to find the body of Corporal Rosa, which was recovered on 17 May. There was an exchange of fire with the guerrillas in the vicinity but no casualties were reported. Subversives Eduardo José Monteiro Teixeira, Danilo Carneiro, José Genoíno Neto and Rioko Kayano were captured in separate incidents when they tried to leave the area. Corporal Odílio Cruz Rosa received a funeral with honours from the Brazilian Army in the city of Belém, at the base of the 5th Guards Company, and was then buried in the Santa Isabel Cemetery.

Operação Cigana (Operation Gipsy)

A group of 15 Army troops left Brasília on 11 April 1972 on a FAB Douglas C-47 for a joint operation of the CIEX, the Planalto Military Command and the 3rd Infantry Brigade, led by CIEX Lieutenant Colonel Carlos Sérgio Torres. They took the subversive prisoner Pedro Albuquerque with them, landing in Araguaína and then travelled to Xambioá in trucks. Albuquerque was there in order to guide the members of the mission to locate more guerrillas in the area, but he proved very uncooperative. He even tried to commit suicide so as not to betray his comrades but was taken to a hospital and recovered. Little or nothing was achieved through his 'assistance' and he had to be taken back to Brasília showing what were said to be signs of insanity.

Military Deployment in Araguaia

Once the presence of guerrillas in the Araguaia area was confirmed, the high command of the Brazilian Armed Forces deployed the units shown in Table 11 to the region.[4]

TABLE 11: Units Deployed to Araguaia
Presidential Guard Battalion – Brasília
CIEX (Army Intelligence Centre)
8th Anti-Aircraft Artillery Group
Guard Cavalry Regiment
Army Military Police – Brasília
10th Hunting Battalion – Brasília
6th Hunting Battalion – Ipameri
36th Infantry Battalion – Uberlândia
Amazónia Military Command – Belém
Jungle Operations and Antiguerrilla Actions Command (COSAG)
PARA-SAR (Paratroopers Brigade)
Roraima Border Command Troops
12° Military Region
1°& 2° Jungle Infantry Battalions (BIS)
3rd Infantry Brigade
FAB Command
1° FAB Air Zone – Belém
2° FAB Air Zone – Brasília
3° FAB Air Zone – Rio de Janeiro
CENIMAR (Navy Information Centre)
Marine Corps Special Group
Federal Police
Military Police – Goiás, Pará, Maranhão, Mato Grosso

Operação Papagaio (Operation Parrot)

When General Emílio Garrastazú Médici assumed the Presidency of Brazil, troops were ordered to be sent to the Araguaia area. Generals Olavo Viana Moog and Antônio Bandeira of the Planalto Military Command (CMP) were appointed as commanders of the armed forces in the first two operations, Parrot and Anaconda. The headquarters of the Criminal Investigation Platoon (PIC), located in the urban military sector of Brasília, was where subversive prisoners were interrogated

For Operation Gipsy, a platoon from the 3rd Infantry Brigade was transported aboard an FAB C-47 to the Araguaia area, taking captured guerrilla Pedro Albuquerque as a guide. (FAB via Hélio Higuchi)

Some of the 300 marines deployed to the Araguaia area during Operation Parrot. (*Corpo de Fuzileiros Navais*)

and tortured, with General Bandeira commanding the repressive apparatus in the Brazilian Army.

Operation Parrot was carried out between April and October 1972. It was the largest military operation carried out by Brazilian military forces after the Second World War, with the deployment of 3,000 effectives, including 300 marines. Vice Admiral Edmundo Drummond Bittencourt, commander of the Marine Corps, had entrusted Corvette Captain Uriburu Lobo da Cruz with the formation of an Operational Group of Marines (FFE) to the fighting in Araguaia.

A gigantic logistical structure was set up in the city of Xambioá, located on the banks of the Araguaia River, in the state of Goiás. The Army troops used local guides, whether peasants or aborigines of the Suruí ethnic group, to pass through the jungle.

The government forces first simultaneously attacked the facilities of detachments A and C, and a few days later turned their attention to Detachment B and the facilities of the guerrilla Military Commission. The troops came from the cities of Marabá and Xambioá. Initially, the Army carried out actions to destroy the guerrilla support structure, such as food depots.

Some 2,700 Army troops were sent to the Araguaia area for Operation Parrot. During patrols in the jungle, they had to cross rivers in small boats. (*Exército Brasileiro*)

The FAB's Aerotactic Operations Command (COMAT) that was formed for the actions in Araguaia assigned three De Havilland

Army soldiers pose with a FAB Bell UH-1H helicopter in the Amazon jungle (left). General Antônio Bandeira (right). (Open source)

Some types of FAB aircraft deployed during Operation Parrot: DHC-5 Buffalo (top) and Douglas C-47 (bottom). (FAB via Hélio Higuchi and José de Alvarenga)

A pair of FAB Cessna L-19 Bird Dogs together with a Bell H-13 (top) and a FAB Bell UH-1H in a landing zone in the Amazon (bottom). (FAB via Hélio Higuchi and José de Alvarenga)

At the beginning of Operation Parrot, COMAT deployed five North American T-6D Texan attack aircraft, armed with MGs, rockets and napalm bombs. (FAB)

A FAB EMRA North American T-6D Texan armed with bombs and rockets. (FAB)

Army troops established checkpoints along the Trans-Amazonian Highway to prevent the escape of the guerrillas. (*Exército Brasileiro*)

Canada DHC-5 Buffalos, one Douglas C-47, five North American T-6D Texans, four Cessna L-19 Bird Dogs and four Bell UH-1Ds to Operation Parrot. The aircraft were employed to transport troops, supplies and ammunition, as well as evacuate dead and wounded troops following combat. If they could not land near the troops, they would drop supplies into combat areas. The aircraft also carried out reconnaissance flights and controlled civil air traffic in the region.

The armed T-6Ds belonged to the Mixed Armed Reconnaissance Squadron (EMRA), and were used in an attack on Serra das Andorinhas, where they dropped several incendiary (napalm) bombs. Only after the mission was it found that there were no guerrillas in the area. The UH-1D helicopters, which were armed with two Browning .30 machine guns to strafe guerrilla positions, also deployed troops to specific areas, always supported by L-19 observation planes. The L-19s were used as forward air controllers (FAC), whose difficult task was to locate the guerrillas in the thick jungle; when they found suspected insurgents, they called either the armed UH-1D helicopters or the T-6Ds to strafe and bomb the area.

The Army's Parachute Brigades, commanded by Major Thaumaturgo Sotero Vaz, patrolled the urban streets, farms, country roads, villages and along the rivers in the area. Major Sotero Vaz flew over the region to coordinate and control actions in the area and also commanded the 1st Jungle Infantry Battalion in operations against the guerrillas.

On 12 April 1972, the military began to enter the region between Marabá and Xambioá, initially with a small team of five men, a group of CIEX personnel led by Major Lício Maciel, followed soon after by battalions of 400 men stationed in each city. The first confrontation between the guerrillas and government troops took place that day, involving elements of the guerrilla Detachment B, near the town of Santa Cruz, with an Army sergeant being killed and a soldier injured. A week later, a second clash took place in the Água Bonita area, where another soldier was wounded.

Bases were installed in the interior, and by August a total of 1,500 troops were involved. Masking their real intentions, the story was spread that this was an exercise by the Fourth Army, whose headquarters were in Recife, 1,600km away. Within this mass of regular infantry soldiers were CIEX men and paratroopers, whose mission was to destroy the guerrillas. It was the beginning of the first of three phases of the military campaign, with three small operations to collect information and survey the area before the arrival of the bulk of the troops.

Checkpoints were set up along the Trans-Amazonian Highway and an air base was established in Xambioá. A command post was installed in a blue-roofed house, on the banks of the Itacaiúnas River, which was called *Casa Azul* (the Blue House). The first attacks on guerrilla bases captured materials used by the guerrillas but failed to find any of the subversives as upon learning of the presence of the Army, the guerrillas disappeared into the forests. For many of them, however, the feeling was that their time was up.

The unexpected launch of the military operation meant the PCdoB insurgents lost the element of surprise, one of the main weapons of any guerrilla combat force. The group with 71 men and women spread across three detachments – A, B and C – in the jungle, was poorly armed, each of them had only a revolver with 40 bullets, and their total armament was limited to 25 rifles, four submachine guns – two of them homemade – 30 shotguns and four hunting carbines. Facing them were almost 2,000 troops armed with FAL rifles and submachine guns. Furthermore, the guerrilla arsenal was of poor quality, and many weapons jammed when fired. One of the guerrillas, after being captured, testified that to hit a target in a tree with her rifle, she needed to aim three trees ahead.

On the afternoon of 5 May, a small patrol searching for information was ambushed near a stream. The guerrillas attacked, dispersing the troops. A lieutenant and a sergeant of the Army paratroopers were wounded in an intense shootout. In a further clash, another soldier

Three guerrillas killed in combat: from left to right, Bergson Gurjão Farias (known as *Jorge*), Kleber Lemos da Silva (known as *Carlito*) and María Lúcia Petit da Silva (known as *Maria*), who were ambushed by Army paratroopers (above). One of the few known photos of guerrillas killed by the Army (below). (Open source)

died and a sergeant was injured. By 1973–1974, in the third and final campaign of the war, the military began to adopt the guerrilla practice of leaving the bodies of slaughtered enemy fighters unburied in the forests. Seeing what was happening, a guide called China – a *caboclo* from the region and recruited by the Army – fearing subsequent reprisal, decided to stay out of the fighting by entering the bush, hiding for two days and disappearing from the Araguaia region.

Local peasant guides who were not sympathetic to the guerrillas were cited in FAB reports explaining the reasons for the regular troops' difficulties in the jungle. According to them, the Army troops made a lot of noise and left many tracks that could be followed by the subversives. They also largely kept to roads and trails and used helicopters, so the guerrillas knew in advance of their approach.

The biggest initial victory of the government forces went largely unnoticed. Once they came under attack by the Brazilian Army, the guerrilla commander-in-chief, João Amazonas, and Elza Monnerat (known as *Dona Maria*), general organiser of the guerrilla structure, kept their forces out of areas in Araguaia where troops operated.

In this first operation, the Army managed to locate and inflict damage on just one of the detachments, C, which comprised only a quarter of the total number of combatants. Money was offered to the *caboclos* for information about the *Paulistas*, enough to buy a large piece of land. Several insurgents were thus located, arrested or killed. The first to fall was Bergson Gurjão Farias (known as *Jorge*), who was betrayed by a peasant. Farias, a former chemistry student at the Federal University of Ceará, become the first person to 'disappear' in Araguaia. Ambushed by a patrol of paratroopers, he was killed by machine-gun fire. His body was hung upside down from a tree, where his head was kicked by soldiers. Two more guerrillas suffered a similar fate, the economist Kleber Lemos da Silva (known as *Carlito*) and 22-year-old former teacher María Lúcia Petit da Silva (known as *Maria*). The latter, the only woman among the members of the Petit family who fought with the subversives, was killed in an ambush

Many times, both the guerrilla and the Army had to resort to the assistance of local peasants, using their precarious boats to navigate the area's rivers. (Courtesy of Albert Grandolini)

with a gunshot to the chest by a peasant serving the military, João Coioió. She was buried in Xambioá in an anonymous grave, wrapped in a parachute and with her head covered with plastic. Her bones, discovered in 1991, were identified by Unicamp (Campinas State University) experts in 1996. She was one of only two dead guerrillas whose body was found and identified.

The collaboration of the region's *caboclos* did not, however, only come from offering money, with some being forced or scared into helping the regime. The Brazilian Armed Forces entered the area as an occupation force, with those accused of trading with the guerrillas being arrested, along with a priest who had spoken out against a mayor and a circus wrestler, the latter because he had long hair. A farmer from Espírito Santo who arrived in Araguaia to take possession of recently purchased land was arrested and thrown for three days into a hole in the ground covered with a wooden lid, inside a camp surrounded by barbed wire where there were already several local residents. A 55-year-old boatman from the region, Lourival Paulino, who had transported the guerrillas across the river, was arrested at the end of May and imprisoned in Xambioá prison, where he died, a death certificate declaring suicide by hanging. A farmer who had given food to the detachment commander *Osvaldão* had his field set on fire and was never seen again.

On 25 May 1972, the Araguaia Guerrilla Forces Command issued its Communiqué No. 1, through which its existence officially became public. This declaration was addressed to the Brazilian people, especially to the peasants of southern Pará, western Maranhão and northern Goiás, where they expressed their resistance against the military regime, the great magnates and the American gringos.[5] It announced the creation of a Union for Freedom and People's Rights (ULPD) to combat hunger, misery, abandonment and oppression.

In June, the subversive José Genoíno, who had been captured by the Army, revealed under torture some important information about the three guerrilla detachments, the Military Commission and the Political Bureau. With this valuable data, the Army was able to plan raids on specific areas to annihilate the guerrillas.

In four months, the Army had managed to arrest or kill fewer than a dozen militants, among them Danilo Carneiro, known as *Nilo*, who had been captured with some peasants when he tried to leave the combat zone. The Army resumed its offensive in September with a force of 3,000 men, but this time in a very different way, trying to win over the people of the region and dissociating itself from the policing approach of the first attack. They landed doctors, dentists and 2.5 tons of medicines in Marabá, leafleted the entire region with messages

The guerrilla José Genoino, captured by the Army in June 1972. (Open Source)

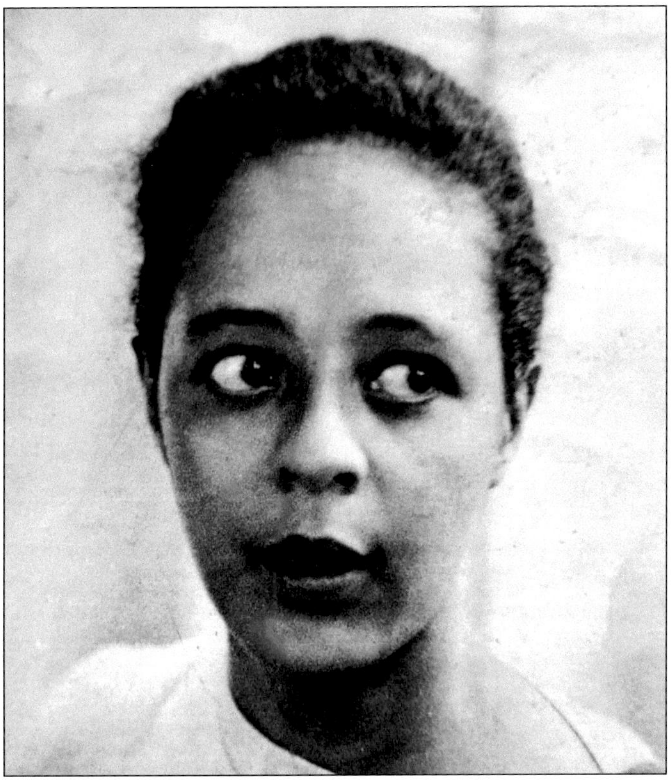

The guerrilla Helenira Rezende de Souza (known as *Fátima*) was captured and executed on 29 September 1972. (Open source)

from captured guerrillas and forced farmers to recognise the labour rights of their employees. Two important victories were achieved by the regime's forces in September, with the death of João Carlos Haas Sobrinho (known as *Dr Juca*), a commander and medical doctor of the guerrilla movement, who was killed in combat, and Helenira Resende (known as *Fátima*), a member of Detachment C, who was executed after being captured. Resende was wanted throughout the country and had a death sentence imposed on her in São Paulo by police chief Sérgio Fleury.

The second stage of the offensive, however, had even worse overall results than the first for the government forces. Scheduled to last 20 days, it only lasted 10. During this period, the guerrillas attacked a base of the 2nd Jungle Infantry Battalion and killed Sergeant Mário Abrahim da Silva. The help of paid bushmen did not lead to any major ambushes of insurgents. The FAB dropped incendiary bombs on three areas of the jungle. A guerrilla fighter was beginning to make a name for herself in the countryside: Dinalva Oliveira Teixeira, known as

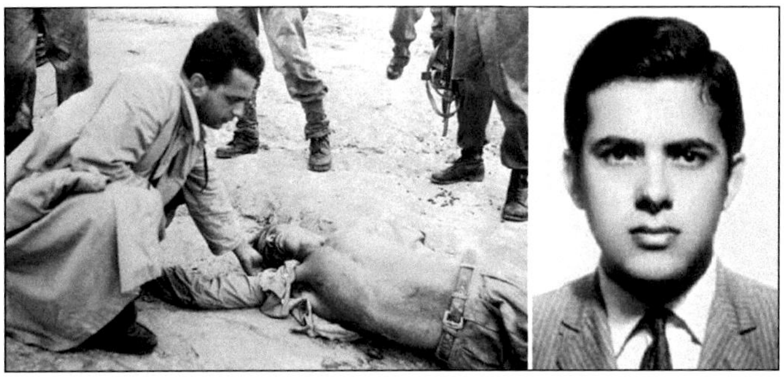

Guerrilla Miguel Pereira Dos Santos aka Cazuza, killed by Brazilian Navy Marines on 20 September 1972. (Courtesy of Albert Grandolini)

Dina, a former Bahian geologist who had become a midwife in the region. She had survived three battles and faced a group of soldiers alone, escaping with a wound to the neck while shooting parachutist Captain Álvaro Pinheiro in the shoulder. Captain Pinheiro was the son of the commander of the National Information School, General Ênio Pinheiro. The Brazilian Armed Forces had a special determination to find Teixeira, considering her a threat to military action in the region, with the aim of destroying the myth created among the people of Araguaia and demoralising the guerrillas.

Disguising the operation as a routine military manoeuvre did more harm than good. The government prevented the publication of PCdoB manifestos, but the party distributed leaflets throughout Araguaia, which reached as far as the south of the region. On 1 August, General Viana Moog delegated to General Antonio Bandeira of the 3rd Infantry Brigade the execution of actions against the communists in the jungle.

For its part, the Navy established a navigation control base in the Remanso dos Botos area, south of Xambioá, on the Araguaia River on 13 September 1972. Some 200 marines were deployed to the base, occupying the left bank of the river, where they built their barracks and established a defensive perimeter in case of an incursion by the guerrillas. This detachment was very well armed with assault rifles, grenades and even mortars. During the day, they inspected all boats that navigated the river, and night navigation was prohibited. Many of these marines participated in ambushes of the guerrillas in the Crentes region and in Igarapé dos Perdidos, managing to kill eight subversives.

On 24 September, the newspaper *O Estado de São Paulo* published a long article about the military manoeuvres in the region, circumventing government censorship of news about troop movements. Two days later, details of the Brazilian guerrilla war were reported in *The New York Times*.

On 29 September, four guerrillas – known as *Vítor*, *António*, *Dina* and *Zé Francisco* – were looking for food in the Pau Preto region when they were surrounded by Army troops. During a firefight, Víctor and *Zé Francisco* were killed, while Antonio and *Dina* were wounded. Although *Dina* managed to escape, *António* was captured and executed. Several days later, marines killed three more guerrillas – *Flávio*, *Juca* and *Gil* – although their colleagues *Raúl* and *Walk* managed to escape.

According to an official statement (Information No. 20/1972 of 3 October), the Army reported the death of 10 guerrillas. Later that month, the troops withdrew from the area. Although the guerrillas were still operational, their casualties had been significant. Between April and October, they lost 19 combatants, eight being killed in action and four murdered after being captured, the other seven being arrested and transferred to Brasília. The Army never officially declared the number of soldiers killed or injured. General Viana Moog left the region speaking of victory and declaring that the success of the operation had exceeded his expectations.

Paratrooper NCOs with their German Shepherd dogs pose in front of several FAB DHC-5 Buffalos and C-119s. Paratroopers were deployed in the Araguaia area. (*Exército Brasileiro*)

A Brazilian Army soldier aiming his rifle in the middle of the Amazon jungle. The combat conditions in such locations were extremely precarious. (EB)

It is interesting to note that the fighting against the guerrillas took place in the middle of the jungle, where it was impossible to use tanks, armoured vehicles and artillery – not even jeeps or trucks, and trails had to be opened in order to reach the guerrilla camps. Troops were deployed either on foot, by helicopters or boats to the combat zone. Consequently, the soldiers only had their assault rifles, submachine guns, hand grenades and, on some occasions, mortars. Furthermore, as has already been noted, aerial reconnaissance was very difficult due to the thickness of the jungle, but even so, it was carried out and that made possible numerous air raids against the guerrillas.

Another important factor was that the military carried out civic action missions among the local population, with medical and dental assistance, the distribution of food and supplies for schools in order to obtain the support of civilians. The guerrillas had done something similar, although on a smaller scale, in the years before the operation. During Operation Parrot, military doctors treated some 7,740 people, Army dentists treated 2,397 patients, and 5,035 people were vaccinated against yellow fever and 2,703 against smallpox. The doctors also assisted dehydrated children, helped women in childbirth, treated people with burns and evacuated the seriously ill to Goiânia and Brasília. Military pharmacies provided free medication to the population. In the area of education, Army professors provided courses for teachers in the region, while farmers and ranchers were assisted by agricultural experts and veterinarians, who treated cases of brucellosis, foot-and-mouth disease and carbuncles in livestock. Within just a few months, the Army thus did much more than the guerrillas had done in several years.

Operation Parrot ended in early October 1972, the Army having carried out its largest mobilisation of troops since the Brazilian Expeditionary Force campaign in Italy during the Second World War. Larger than three of the four expeditions against Canudos in the late nineteenth century, it had enjoyed a numerical advantage of 50-to-1, but the Araguaia Guerrilla remained in existence. The conventional use of large regular military units in the first campaign against the guerrillas ended with the departure of the troops due to the ineffectiveness of such an approach. The saturation of the region by conventional troops led only to the disorganisation of the intervention force. The indecisive clashes with the guerrillas lowered the morale of the military, especially among the marine infantry units, which were therefore exempt from further operations. However, this conventional operation had already set a distinctive mark for the entire campaign in the sense that it was carried out in a brutal manner. Not all troops were removed from the area, with three Army platoons left behind in the regions of Caianos, Abóbora and Xambioá. Aerial operations by the FAB, the 2° and 3° ERA Squadrons flew missions for more than 414 hours, and two FAB Lockheed C-130 Hercules were used to transport marines back to their bases.

Despite managing to inflict some casualties on the insurgents, the results of the operation were not as good as expected. It was found that some of the equipment being used (from types of uniforms to weapons) was unsuitable for such confrontations. The lack of information about their opponents made operations very difficult, and the presence of uniformed contingents intimidated the local population rather than persuading them to provide information. It became evident that an improved survey of the enemy by intelligence agencies was necessary in order to act more effectively. The final balance of Operation Parrot was 13 guerrillas killed and 10 captured, against two Army personnel killed and four wounded. In addition, the Army reported three deaths and three injuries due to accidents.

Army Colonel Álvaro de Souza Pinheiro, assigned to the General Staff of the Brazilian Armed Forces – one of the first military officers

A FAB Lockheed C-130E taking off, carrying Brazilian Navy Marines back to their bases in October 1972. (Courtesy of Albert Grandolini)

to publish his own conclusions of the operation decades later – highlighted five 'series of mistakes' that were made:

- Misconception at the operational and tactical levels. In jungle terrain, Army patrols were restricted to moving in platoons of between 35 and 40 men along trails, while smaller guerrilla groups numbering between five and 10 could move through the jungle. Therefore, the initial actions proved extremely ineffective.
- Lack of unity of command, caused above all by the fact that the Marabá combat base was under the control of the Amazon Military Command, while Xambioá was controlled by the Planalto Military Command.
- Deficient information about the terrain and the enemy. There were no credible maps or aerial photographs of the region of operations. There was widespread lack of knowledge of the terrain. This resulted in patrols moving only along trails, while the guerrillas, who had in-depth knowledge of the terrain, could easily pass through the jungle.
- Great diversity of units employed and deficiencies in training. Units from different parts of the country were employed in the campaign, some of them having serious deficiencies in training in counter-guerrilla operations in a jungle environment. Many of the units involved comprised recently recruited, ill-trained soldiers.
- Lack of continuity in operations. Unlike the guerrilla force that had already been in the area for some years and remained there, the troops were employed for predetermined periods of no more than 20 days, after which they returned to their headquarters without being replaced.

The President of Brazil, General of the Army Emílio Garrastazú Médici. (Open source)

Nevertheless, General Emílio Médici's government was determined to wipe out the guerrilla forces. In 1973, the elite professional soldiers of the country's armed forces entered the scene. The guerrillas released a statement stating that the dictatorship's troops 'fled in terror' before the 'great' revolutionary force, but nothing could be further from the truth, as government forces returned with fresh tactics and ended up annihilating the guerrillas.

Meanwhile, secret agents from the FAB's Aeronautics Information Centre (*Centro de Informações da Aeronáutica*/CISA) dedicated themselves to monitoring the activities of the communist guerrillas. They had identified movements in the vicinity of Xambioá, São

Army Captain Sebastião Rodrigues de Moura (right), known as *Curió* or *Doctor Luchini* during Operation Anaconda. His fake identity was that of an INCRA assistant technician. (Open source)

A FAB Cessna L-19E Bird Dog with the fake civil registration PT-DCB on the runway at Xambioá. The pilot, a FAB officer, was in civilian clothes, with long hair and beard. (Col. Pedro Corrêa Cabral via Hélio Higuchi)

Geraldo, Gameleira, Santa Cruz and Palestina. They discovered that *Osvaldão* and about 11 guerrillas visited farmers to indoctrinate them and add them to their logistics chain. They also identified *Dina* and eight guerrillas in the Pau Preto region, where they bought rice from farmers. The FAB spies also identified peasants who collaborated with the guerrillas, whose names were included in a report to the Armed Forces High Command.

Operação Sucuri (Operation Anaconda)

An intelligence operation that lasted from April–October 1973, the planning of Operation Anaconda was in the hands of Lieutenant Colonel Carlos Sérgio Torres and Major Gilberto Airton Zenkner of the CIEX. The Army High Command selected 32 men (seven officers, nine sergeants and 16 corporals and soldiers) from the Brasília DOI and the 3rd Motorized Infantry Brigade for the operation, along with 21 civilians. Although General António Bandeira was nominally in command, the operation was in the hands of Lieutenant Colonel Torres. The conflict zone was divided into two areas – Xambioá and the Trans-Amazonian Highway. For this operation, both the civilians and the military involved were prohibited from any offensive action against the guerrillas, and they were to be disguised as peasant settlers at all times. Furthermore, they all had false identities and did not carry any type of official documentation with them. Codenames were chosen for the participants in the operation: General Bandeira was known as *Camilo* or *Doctor Pedrinho*, while Major Zenker was *Uncle António* and Captain Aluísio Madruga de Moura e Souza, who was an agriculturalist, went under the name *Doctor Melo*. Besides them, Captain Sebastião Rodrigues de Moura was known as *Curió*, and also as *Doctor Luchini*, a pseudo-agronomist from the National Institute of Colonisation and Agrarian Reform (INCRA) settled in Xambioá. Instead of the ostentation of Operation Parrot, the soldiers arrived in disguise, dressed as civilians.

The Army intended to successfully employ the same infiltration techniques as the guerrillas. The members of this mission were divided into three teams – A, B and C – each with specific areas of influence. The information obtained would be sent first to the coordinator of each team and then to the general coordinator. To avoid previous errors, an extensive information network was set up by the armed forces. Military intelligence agents infiltrated the local population disguised as farmers, mining engineers, agronomists and traders. Within a few months, enough information was obtained to launch another military operation, this time decisively. There are no references to offensive operations by FAB aircraft during this period, although some Cessna L-19 Bird Dogs and Bell UH-1s were used for logistics

A FAB UH-1H helicopter, with all military identification marks overpainted, in Xambioá. (Col. Pedro Corrêa Cabral via Hélio Higuchi)

The Brazilian Air Force still had several PBY-5A Catalinas in active service, which normally operated in the Amazon area in the 1970s. (Courtesy of Albert Grandolini)

The Police and the Armed Forces arrested numerous people linked to the PCdoB in several states of Brazil and seized a large amount of printed material of a communist nature, undermining the guerrilla's logistical bases. (Courtesy of Albert Grandolini)

support with all the FAB markings overpainted, and in some cases with fake civil registrations.

Men disguised as *caboclos* opened roadside wineries, became garlic traders, bought fields, opened bakeries and small logging companies, and one even sold ammunition to the guerrillas so as not to arouse suspicion. They had all previously been introduced to rural life, spending time on farms around Brasília. The new 'residents' wrote down information about what they saw and movements in the area, identifying the guerrillas and peasants who had contact with them. Meanwhile, *Curió* took a PBY Catalina flying boat across the river on the weekends to collect their reports. Between April and October, the guerrilla movement was mapped, with names catalogued, and *caboclos* and peasants linked to the subversives were identified. In April, a confidential report was prepared containing 51 names of residents of the region who were suspected of collaborating with the guerrillas. By September, the list was increased to 400 names.

In the first half of 1973, the guerrilla forces were reorganised, with stores of supplies and ammunition scattered in shelters throughout the jungle. They recruited two more collaborators from among the region's residents and formed 13 clandestine support groups, totalling 39 people. They killed three military collaborators, one of them a local gunman, and attacked a police station on the Trans-Amazonian Highway. They surrounded a police building, set fire to the thatched roof, captured its garrison of five soldiers and then fled, taking their uniforms, six rifles and a revolver. In August, after a trial held in the jungle, the guerrilla leadership shot one of the militants for ideological weakness and adultery. By then, there were a total of 56 subversives – men and women – six of whom were peasants. They suffered from a lack of clothing, shoes and ammunition, and there was no prospect of receiving reinforcements because the PCdoB had already suffered defeats in six states around the country. Yet although weapons remained insufficient, morale was still quite high. The proximity of the rainy season in Araguaia, which would prevent the movement of large vehicles, made the guerrillas assume that the Army would only return at the beginning of 1974.

The official secrecy surrounding everything related to the guerrilla movement was justified by the military as denying the guerrillas the recognition that the Brazilian Armed Forces were being used to deal with a major internal security problem. General Médici feared that the spreading of news of fighting would give notoriety to the guerrillas and transform Araguaia into a 'liberated zone', as had occurred in regions of Southeast Asia.

After completing the intelligence survey through Operation Anaconda, in which tables covered in photographs and biographies of guerrillas and residents were set up in the operations centre in Marabá, soldiers returned to the region in October 1973. Unlike the first attack, which had involved conscripted soldiers and recruits, the troops now had no uniforms and carried no identification papers, wore their hair long and were bearded like the locals, and were made up of experienced men from the Parachute Brigade, Jungle Battalion and Special Forces Battalion who were transported in FAB UH-1 helicopters without military markings. Smaller in number, they were the elite of the Brazilian Armed Forces. State secrecy regarding the struggle in Araguaia led to clandestine actions. Unlike the fight against the armed struggle in the cities, there were no police or military investigations, nor formal complaints or court sentences. The order was to take no prisoners, and no prisoners would be taken.

Operação Marajoara (Operation Marajoara)

General Hugo de Abreu was appointed to lead Operation Marajoara,[6] which was carried out between 7 October 1973 and October 1974. At the beginning of the operation, 300 military personnel were sent to Araguaia disguised as civilians. They were transported to the conflict zone on aircraft from 1° ETA (Esquadrão de Transporte Aéreo, Air Transport Squadron) of Belém and 6° ETA of Brasília. An additional four FAB UH-1D helicopters and four Cessna L-19s were deployed for tactical air support. Much later, a total of 3,202 Army personnel had direct or indirect participation in the operation, and 250 paratroopers from the Army and the FAB were also added. The Military Police of the states of Pará and Goiás manned barricades on the main routes and outside prisons in the area. Through information collected in Operation Anaconda, it was realised that instead of large-scale operations, it would be more effective to use reduced contingents divided into several platoons in incursions into the jungle. For radio messages, the code 'Papa-Mike' was established to identify the guerrillas, 'Papa' meaning *povo* (people) and 'Mike' meaning *mata* (jungle).

There was great concern about the international repercussions of the operation. The guerrillas transmitted daily information abroad about the movement, which was retransmitted to Brazil, in Portuguese, by a shortwave radio station in Tirana, Albania. The presence of regular troops in armed confrontations within the country could be interpreted as a situation of major internal belligerence, and the

Major General Hugo de Abreu, a veteran of the Second World War Brazilian Expeditionary Force, Commander of the Parachute Infantry Brigade, was in charge of the Army troops in Operation Marajoara (left). During Geisel's military government, he was Chief of the Military Cabinet. On the right, General de Abreu with President Geisel and Ministers Golbery do Couto e Silva, Chief of Staff of the Presidency of the Republic, and Antônio Azeredo da Silveira, Minister of Foreign Affairs (right). (Open source)

The *Casa Azul* (Blue House), headquarters of the CIEX in Marabá, which was also a prison for captured guerrillas and collaborators. (Open source)

guerrillas wanted to obtain international recognition as being involved in a war zone, and consequently be subject to foreign intervention.

It was to avoid such a situation that it was decided that for this operation, the troops would be disguised as civilians, wearing no uniforms that identified them as a regular military force.

The headquarters of the intelligence agency was located in Marabá, alongside the Itacaiúnas River and close to the airport, in the *Casa Azul* facility, which was also used as a prison for captured guerrillas and collaborators. The troops were based in Xambioá, under the guise of working for a timber company.

Meanwhile, at the beginning of the operation, the guerrilla movement had 56 effectives (Detachment A with 22, B with 12 and C with 14, plus the Military Commission with eight). Their armament was insufficient and ammunition scarce. They did not have compasses, batteries or even matches to light fires and cook. There was also little by way of medical supplies, and many of the guerrillas suffered from malaria, yellow fever and diarrhoea. In short, their situation was truly pathetic. The Army, aware of this dire situation, acted first by neutralising the guerrilla's logistical support.

As had been the case in previous operations, aircraft support would be essential, so planes and helicopters from the 1° EMRA Squadron based in Belém do Pará were deployed, as well as four Cessna L-19Es and four Bell UH-1H helicopters. Initially, two UH-1Hs and a pair of L-19Es were based at Marabá, and the rest in Xambioá. However, during the missions, Marabá was left with only one type of

Army soldiers posing in a clearing in the jungle (left). The 'Papa-Mike' guerrillas, the code used by the Brazilian Army for subversives (right). (Open source)

FAB Captain Pedro Corrêa Cabral in civilian clothing in front of his Cessna L-19E with the false civil registration PT-DLO. It appears that the landing gear of the aircraft had sunk in the mud and farmers are helping to move the aircraft. (Pedro Corrêa Cabral via Hélio Higuchi)

Local children and some peasants near a FAB UH-1H with the military markings crudely overpainted in black. The pilot, shirtless and wearing a white cap, leaning on the helicopter was Captain Pedro Corrêa Cabral. (Pedro Corrêa Cabral via Hélio Higuchi)

each aircraft, transferring the others to Xambioá. By the end of the campaign, all eight aircraft were concentrated in Xambioá.

On 7 October 1973, government troops returned to Araguaia. A smaller force, around 300 men, disguised and without uniforms but with a large quantity of weapons, were left in several villages in the area occupied by the guerrillas. Some of them arrived hidden in hollow crates inside trucks transporting timber. As far as the locals were aware, they were employees of *Agropecuária Araguaia* (an agricultural company) and *Mineração Aripuanã* (a mining company), so as not to raise suspicions among the general population or the guerrillas. However, as soon as they arrived, they started arresting residents. Farmers and small traders were taken to prisons in Xambioá and Marabá, where some were held in holes in clearings with gratings over the top. In Tabocão, 17 men were arrested and reports of torture began to appear. Army Captain Aluísio Madruga de Moura e Souza remained a central figure in the repression of the guerrilla movement, carrying out deployments in Marabá, Carolina, Porto Nacional, Xambioá and Belém. His efforts were rewarded with two decorations, the Bronze Military Medal and the Peacemaker Medal.

From the beginning of hostilities, the guerrilla movement underestimated the capacity of the Army and never believed that Federal troops could carry out an effective encirclement in the middle of the jungle. The guerrilla Military Commission then decided to form a single force, uniting all the troops of the three detachments for offensive actions. However, this proved totally ineffective as the Army troops were able to successfully besiege and slowly annihilate the guerrillas.

The Army effectives were organised into small units, having also recruited some locals who had previously collaborated with the guerrillas. These groups searched for guerrilla supply posts providing either food, ammunition or medical supplies, which were systematically destroyed, leaving the insurgents prone to contracting tropical diseases such as yellow fever. This strategy of attrition managed to dismantle the guerrilla movement in Araguaia before it could gain momentum.

All military markings on FAB aircraft deployed to the area were removed and they were given fictitious civil registrations. FAB flight and maintenance personnel wore civilian clothes and were allowed to grow their hair long and have beards to preserve the secrecy of the undercover operation. The UH-1Hs used in these missions originally had the serials FAB-8654, 8655, 8656 and 8657. During the course of the operation, some UH-1Hs were replaced by others, one of them being FAB-8658.

Members of the FAB's 1° EMRA Squadron had been unable to fly for a long time due to a leak in the main rotor hub having been detected in all UH-1H helicopters. To maintain their cover as a mining company in Xambioá, they chose the name Mineradora DDP, with the acronym standing for 'days and days without doing anything', in reference to the months of boredom that had passed without them being able to fly. Once the technical problems were solved with their helicopters, they were able to fly more than 1,000 missions, belying the cover name they had chosen.

According to the testimony of the then Captain Pedro Corrêa Cabral, who was first a FAB Cessna L-19 Bird Dog pilot and was then trained to fly Bell UH-1D/H helicopters, during the Araguaia Guerrilla, a FAB Lockheed P2V-5 Neptune, while on patrol in the Atlantic Ocean northeast of Brazil, intercepted a Soviet merchant ship, which was ordered to proceed to a Brazilian port for cargo inspection. There was a suspicion that the ship was carrying weapons for the guerrillas. When the Soviet crew refused to obey the instruction, the pilot of the Neptune contacted his base and received the order to attack the ship with rockets. However, the pilot did not immediately carry out this order, discovering shortly after that the Soviet ship had a damaged rudder and could thus not sail towards a Brazilian port. Captain Corrêa Cabral was one of the few FAB officers who commented on his experiences in Araguaia in a book he published, but the Brazilian Air Force officially denied his 'revelations'.

In the first two campaigns, *caboclos* were often convinced to collaborate with the military in exchange for cash payments. During Operation Marajoara, the situation was somewhat different, with more than 20 of them becoming Army guides. Zé Catingueiro, a local *caboclo*, had in previous months collaborated with the guerrillas, taking messages from them to civilians inviting them to join the group. Months later, with the arrival of the troops, he killed the guerrilla Jana

The principal amphibious vehicle of the Brazilian Marine Corps during the 1970s was the GMC-Biselli DUWK amphibious truck, 39 of which were purchased from surplus stocks in the USA. Known in Brazil as *Caminhão Anfíbio do Corpo de Fuzileiros Navais* (Marine Corps Amphibious Truck/CAMANF), these were armed with a single 7.62mm machine gun, and could carry either 2,300kg of cargo, or 24 fully-armed marines. (Artwork by David Bocquelet)

In 1969-1970, Engesa rolled out several prototypes designated VBB-1 and VBB-2, all based on the layout of the M8 Greyound. Eventually, these evolved into the VBR-2, which utilised an entirely new hull, but still the same antiquated turret and 37mm cannon. Following additional modification, this resulted in the CRR, which entered series production for the Brazilian Army under the designation EE-9 Cascavel, in the configuration shown here, in 1972-1973. Subsequently, on Portuguese request, Engesa developed a heavily modified variant with an automatic transmission and the ET-90 turret mounting a 90mm low-pressure gun from the Panhard AML armoured car – which became a highly successful export article. Moreover, in parallel, an armoured personnel carrier came into being in form of the EE-11 Urutu. (Artwork by David Bocquelet)

In 1960, within an initiative to upgrade its armed forces, Brazil purchased 386 M41 Walker Bulldog light tanks from surplus US stocks. Delivered in successive shipments over the following seven years, the M41s formed the backbone of the Brazilian Army's armoured formations. They were armed with the 76mm M32A1 gun, a coaxially installed 7.62mm machine gun, and a roof-mounted 12.7mm machine gun. (Artwork by David Bocquelet)

The old B-26 Invaders of the 1°/10° GAV (1st Squadron of the 10th Aviation Group) did not fly direct air strikes against the Araguaia Guerrilla. However, during Operation Fish III, in May 1972, they flew maritime patrols along the coast of the Atlantic Ocean, searching for vessels possibly transporting arms and other supplies. All the surviving aircraft were overhauled in the USA and received a new camouflage pattern making them outwardly similar in appearance to famous B-26Ks. Moreover, since 1970, their designation was switched from B-26 to A-26. All of these changes are clear on this A-26C, shown as of around 1972, by when it received the large red number '10', outlined in white, on the vertical fin. (Artwork by Tom Cooper)

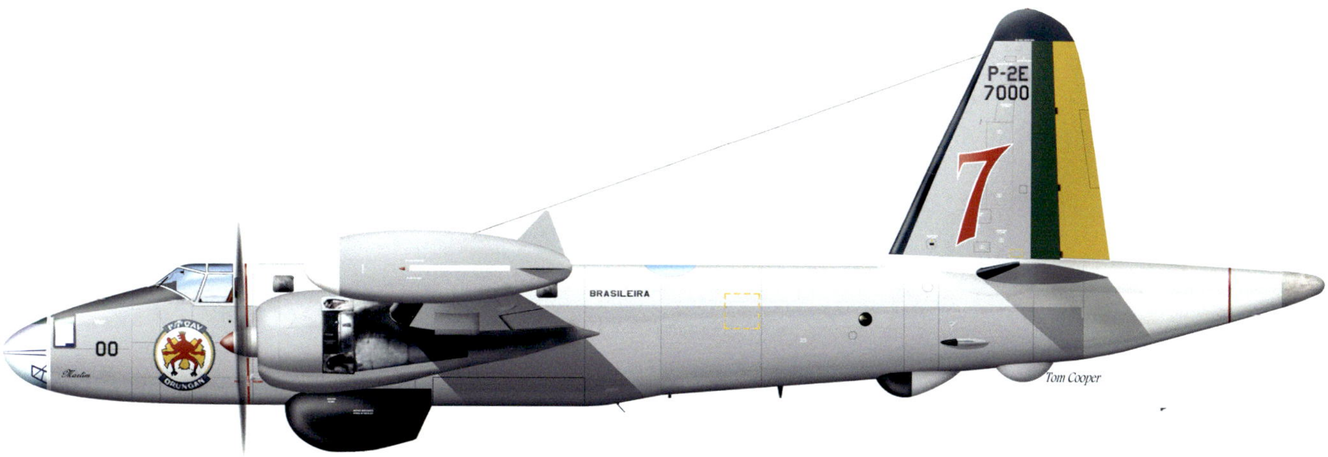

Lockheed P2V-5 (P-2E) Neptune maritime patrol aircraft of the Salvador-based 1°/7° GAV also patrolled the Brazilian coast of the Atlantic Ocean for weeks. In March 1972, they intercepted the Soviet merchant *Yuri Gagarin*, underway in Brazilian territorial waters to monitor rockets tested at the Barreira de Inferno launch centre. They also participated in Operation Fish III. By that time, they were re-designated the P-2E, repainted in white and light aircraft grey, and became known as Netuno in Brazil. This was the serial number 7000 (ex-RAF WX505), which was one of the Neptunes known to have worn the names of sea birds or fish: in this case *Martim*, applied in black, low on the left side of the nose. (Artwork by Tom Cooper)

Another old type still in service with the FAB as of early 1970, and to see deployment against the guerrilla was the Bell 47G Sioux. Starting in 1958, a total of 49 light helicopters were acquired in sub-variants 47D1 and 47G2, and deployed as trainers. During the COIN campaign they were primarily operated in the liaison and observation roles, frequently in conjunction with L-19Es. The majority of the fleet was painted in yellow: they wore FAB titles low on the cabin, black serials on their fuel tanks, and national colours across the fin. (Artwork by Luca Canossa)

Between 1957 and 1980, the FAB acquired an operated a total of nine Stinson L-9A Voyager and 11 Cessna L-19E Bird Dog liaison aircraft. All were painted in dark green overall, but wore the Brazilian national colours on their rudders. This L-19E (serial FAB 3156) was operated by the 3°Esquadrão Águia (also 3° EMRA, or the 'Eagle Squadron'), home-based in Santa Cruz. During counterinsurgency operations against the Araguaia Guerrilla, the type was mainly deployed by Forward Air Controllers: usually equipped with four tubes for 2.25-inch (68mm) unguided rockets used to mark targets. (Artwork by Tom Cooper)

This L-19E was assigned to the 1° EMRA (the 'Falcon Squadron'), but had all of its national markings and the usual set of FAB-insignia overpainted: while retaining its dark green overall livery, it received a fake civilian registration PT-DCB, crudely applied in white on the rear fuselage. This was the finish in which it was deployed within the framework of Operation Marajoara, against the Araguaia Guerrilla, from October 1973 until October 1974. (Artwork by Tom Cooper)

During the 1940s and 1960s, Brazil acquired no fewer than 427 North American T-6 training aircraft. The majority belonged to the T-6D sub-variant and was operated in bare metal overall: they wore only blanket FAB serials ranging from 1397 to 1435 and 1447 to 1506. Subsequent acquisitions included SNJ-4s, SNJ-5Cs, and SJN-6s (serials in the range 1600 to 1799), some of which were operated by the Brazilian Navy. Many were locally modified to give them COIN capability, including the installation of a 7.62mm machine gun in front of the cockpit, and one in each wing. Their armament was completed by either up to six or eight underwing hardpoints for bombs up to 25kg each, or two hardpoints for bombs up to 250kg each. (Artwork by Tom Cooper)

During the Second World War, dozens of modified Brazilian T-6Ds were operated by Mixed Reconnaissance & Attack Squadrons and deployed for anti-submarine patrols and convoy protection duties. Through the 1950s close air support, COIN-operations, border patrol, liaison, and reconnaissance were added to their tasks. Based on a decision from the time of the Second World War, such aircraft were – nominally – supposed to wear a standardised camouflage pattern in two shades of green. Eventually, only the aircraft of the ERA-42 were painted that way: the other of armed Brazilian T-6s were painted in a range of different colours. This example (FAB1422) is shown as operated by the ERA-41 ('Vampires Squadron') in 1972-1974. It was armed with wing-mounted machine guns and four locally-manufactured 100kg bombs. (Artwork by Tom Cooper)

This T-6D (serial FAB 1325) was assigned to the 5° EMRA ('Panther Squadron'), and based in Santa Maria. It was one of relatively few to receive its camouflage colours in two shades of green, applied following the standardised pattern from the 1940s. Unlike FAB 1422, where undersurfaces were painted in light blue, FAB 1425 had these overpainted in light grey. The aircraft is shown armed with a total of three 7.62mm machine guns (including one installed in front of the cockpit), and a pair of 100kg bombs. The red band on the latter denoted the incendiary version. (Artwork by Tom Cooper)

By 1972-1974, a number of overhauled T-6Ds were repainted in modern US military colours: this former SNJ, upgraded to the T-6D standard, was assigned to the ERA-41 as of that time. It received a livery in olive drab or forest green on top surfaces and sides (with a deep anti-glare panel in matt black along the top of the forward fuselage), and light aircraft grey on undersurfaces. A large unit patch was applied on the engine cowling; the nickname 'Cumbica' on a red stripe (outlined in yellow) atop of the fin; while the official serial (FAB1616) remained relatively small, and was applied in yellow on the rear fuselage. (Artwork by Tom Cooper)

As of 1973-1975, the 'Falcon Squadron' of the 1° EMRA was also operating Bell UH-1H Huey helicopters. Brazil acquired a total of 54 of these, starting in 1972 but – contrary to the usual practice of many other operators of this prolific type – the FAB went to some lengths in regards of their camouflage colours. Except for few UH-1Ds of the 1° EMRA operated from Belém as of 1973-1974, most had a three-tone, wrap-around, disruptive pattern in tan and two shades of green. During the Araguaia War, they were deployed to transport troops, but also conducted search-and-rescue operations, casualty- and medical evacuations, and were utilised in the assault role. (Artwork by Luca Canossa)

This UH-1H (serial number FAB 8536) was assigned to the 'Panther Squadron' of the 5° EMRA, home-based in Santa Maria. This was probably the busiest FAB unit of the Araguaia War: its UH-1Ds and UH-1Hs were deployed in assault and troop-carrying roles, and frequently armed with pods for unguided 37mm or 68mm rockets, or with two pintle-mounted 7.62mm machine guns (one on each side of the cabin). (Artwork by Luca Canossa)

A number of UH-1Ds retained their olive drab overall livery (applied prior to delivery) throughout the early years of service with the FAB. This example is known to have been assigned to the Belém-based 'Falcon Squadron' of the 1° EMRA when deployed in the Araguaia region for Operation Marajoara, conducted between October 1973 and October 1974. It had its FAB markings crudely overpainted with black or dark green, and no visible civilian registrations. (Artwork by Luca Canossa)

The FAB was one of the earliest customers for Bell 206A helicopters, purchasing the first seven in 1967. Four of these (serials 8580 to 8583) were designated OH-4 and operated in liaison and observation roles with the 5th Mixed Reconnaissance and Attack Squadron, and is how they were deployed against the Araguaia Guerrilla. Notably, atop of their olive drab overall livery, during the operations of 1972-1975, they had a camouflage pattern in light green – together with a complete set of national markings, serials, and unit insignia. (Artwork by Tom Cooper)

In 1965, the FAB selected the de Havilland Canada DHC-5A Caribou/Buffalo as a replacement for old Fairchild C-82 Packet transports then still in service with the 1°/1° Gropo de Transporte de Tropa. Deliveries of a total of 24 aircraft (serials 2350 to 2373) began in 1968, and they received the Brazilian designation C-115. Nicknamed 'Búfalo' in FAB service, they were originally operated with their top surfaces in white, and the lower portion of the fuselage, fin, and undersides in medium grey. A portion of the skin on the left side of the port engine cowling on this example (serial number 2369) seems to have been replaced, and it received the 'parrot head' insignia on the fin. (Artwork by Tom Cooper)

In 1964, Brazil acquired three SC-130Es (serials 2450 to 2452) for search and rescue purposes. They were operated by the 1°/6° Grupo from Recife AB, and – in addition to a livery in white and grey, similar to that applied on C-115 Bufalos – wore markings clearly distinguishing their SAR- and reconnaissance roles. Five 'vanilla' C-130E transports (serials 2453 to 2457) and three additional SC-130Es (serials 2458 to 2460) followed between 1965 and 1969, of which the former were assigned to the 1°/1° Grupo, the insignia of which was applied above the front entry doors, as illustrated here. Except for 2450 and 2452 (written off in earlier accidents), all saw deployment in support of operations against the Araguaia Guerrilla of 1972-1974. (Artwork by Tom Cooper)

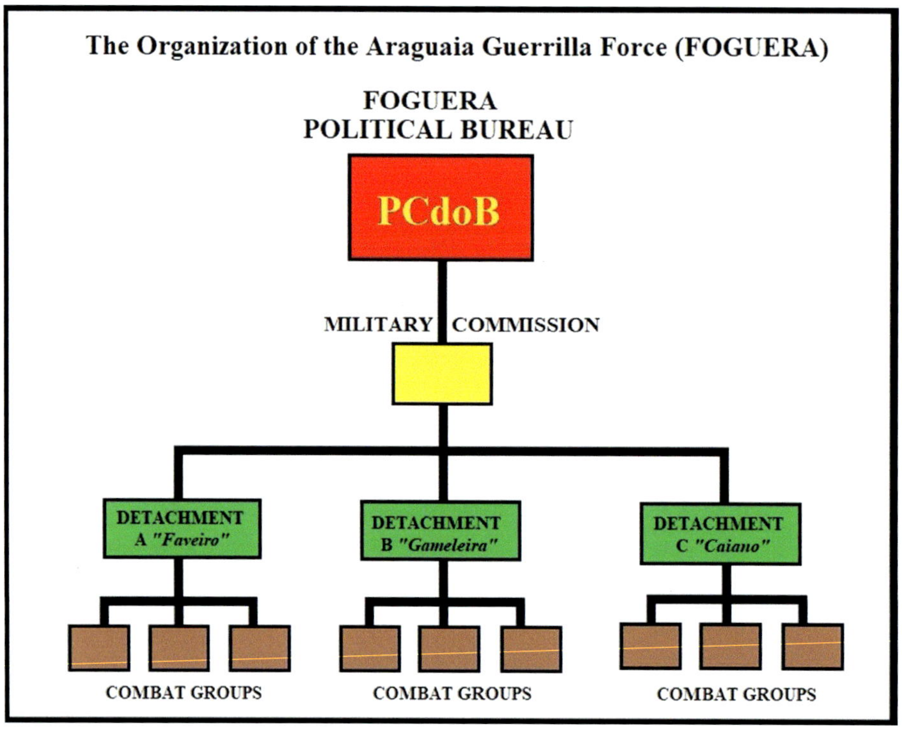

(Diagram by author)

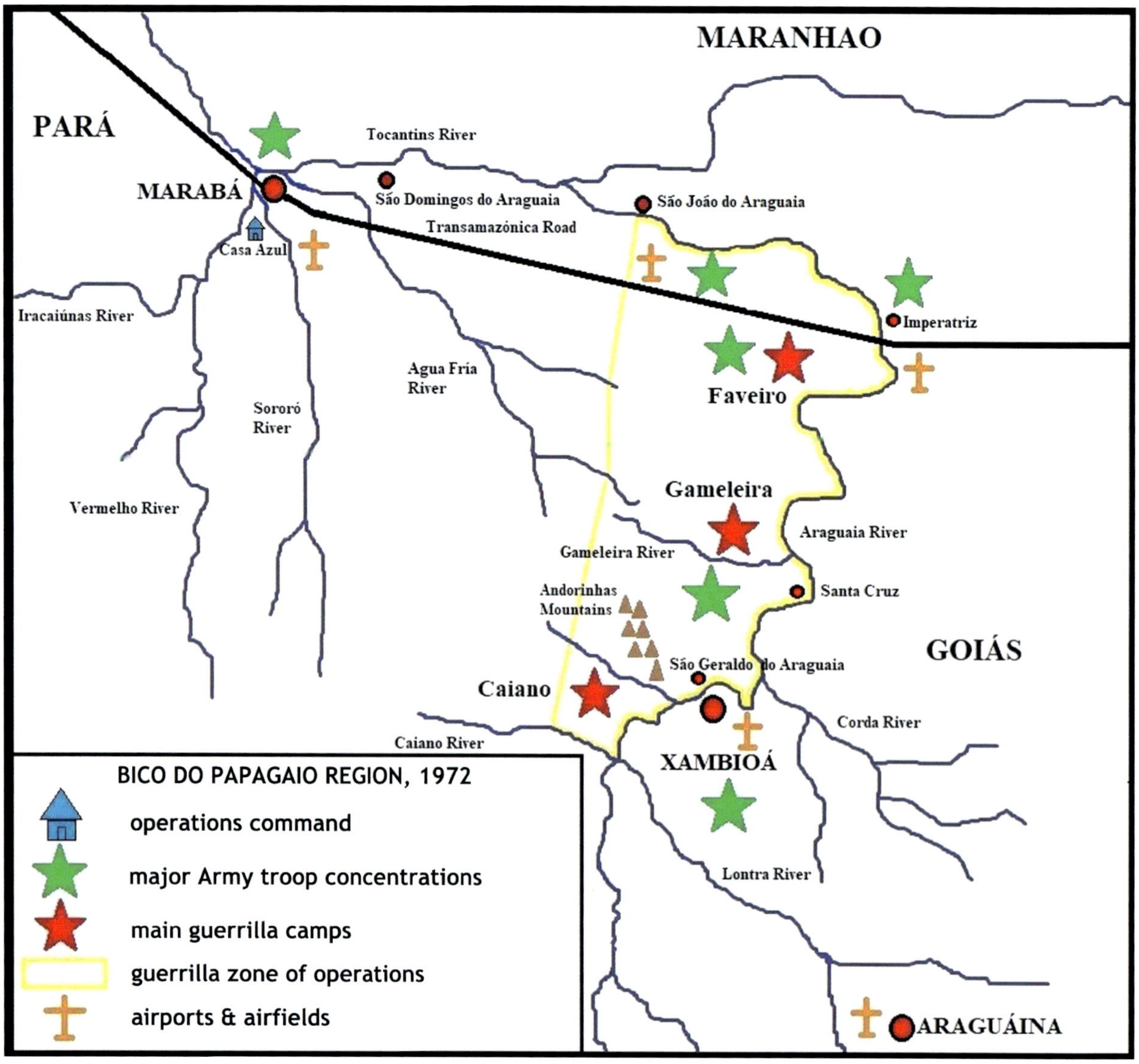

(Map by author)

(Maps by author)

A FAB Lockheed P2V-5 Neptune (top), while on patrol in the Atlantic Ocean northeast of Brazil, intercepted a Soviet merchant ship (bottom), which was ordered to proceed to a Brazilian port for cargo inspection. (FAB)

Moroni, known as *Cristina*. One local resident, 40-year-old Ângelo Lopes de Souza, knew of the guerrillas and the places they normally went on patrol. He was detained by the Army and taken to the Bacaba base, where he spent a month in prison. He accepted an offer to guide the military forces, realising that otherwise he would probably have been killed. As a result, in retaliation for him helping the Army, the village of Água Boa in São Domingos do Araguaia was completely burned down by guerrillas.

The arrival of CIEX effectives and elite troops in the region resulted in a voluntary curfew among residents, with nobody leaving their home at night. The military strategy of intimidation provoked support for both sides in the conflict; to the government forces, out of fear, and to the guerrillas, to escape the military. Those who sided with the subversives included students in Jana Moroni's literacy classes and Maria Célia Corrêa (known as *Rosa*), a former bank clerk from Rio and a philosophy student at the Federal University of Rio de Janeiro (UFRJ).

In mid-October 1973, Major Lício Maciel commanded a team made up of Major Alberico, Sergeant Cid, five soldiers and a civilian. Hearing gunshots, they headed to an area where they found five guerrillas who had just killed two pigs. In the subsequent combat, the subversives *Zé Carlos*, *Zebão* and *Alfredo* were killed, while *Nunes* was wounded was captured. The latter was taken by helicopter to the *Casa Azul*, where he was executed. The only one of the guerrillas to escape was João Araguaia. On 24 October, an Army patrol found guerrilla Lúcia Maria de Sousa, known as *Sónia*, and a peasant named Wilson in the jungle and a firefight broke out in which the insurgent was wounded and the peasant escaped. The patrol's commanding officer, Major Lício Maciel, made the mistake of approaching *Sónia*, who fired her revolver, wounding him in the hand and face and also injuring Captain *Curió*. The other troops opened fire and killed *Sónia* before helping their wounded officers.

Between October 1973 and October 1974, the guerrillas were systematically exterminated. Small combat groups of soldiers entered the jungle with more firepower than all the guerrillas combined. The officers and sergeants carried with them a report, 'General Rules of Action – Capture and Destruction Plan', which identified the guerrillas to be killed by priority. The members of the Military Commission were to be the first to be eliminated.

On Christmas Day 1973, the Army located the camp of the guerrilla's Military Commission, thanks to aerial reconnaissance carried out by FAB UH-1Ds and T-6Ds. A combat group was immediately sent and during a shootout the guerrillas Maurício Grabois (known as *Mário*, the combat leader of the PCdoB), Pedro Gil, *Luiz*, *Amaury* and Paulo Rodrigues were killed. The Araguaia Guerrilla was thus decapitated. In a classified Army report written in January 1974, it was stated that by then the guerrillas only had 33 fighters left and that their entire military leadership had been eliminated.

During January 1974, the guerrillas suffered further casualties: Nelson Lima Piauhy Dourado, Rodolfo de Carvalho Troiano, Telma Regina Cordeiro Corrêa, Vandick Reidner Pereira Coqueiro and José Lima Piauhy Dourado. Several days later, Cilon da Cunha Brum (known as *Simão*), who had been captured, was eliminated by the Army. In the following month, Custódio Saraiva Neto, Tobías Pereira Júnior and Antônio Guilherme Ribeiro Ribas were also killed.

From then on, the guerrilla had lost its status as an organised military force, dividing into columns that were gradually decimated over a period of six months. It became a manhunt and a fight for

Some of the guerrillas killed by the Army in October 1973, from left to right: Jana Moroni (known as *Cristina*), João Gualberto Calatroni (known as *Zebão*), André Grabois (known as *Zé Carlos*), Divino Ferreira de Sousa (known as *Nunes*) and Lúcia María de Sousa (known as *Sónia*). (Open source)

The eight guerrillas killed during an Army ambush on 25 December 1973. Top, from left to right: Maurício Grabois (known as *Mário*), Antonio Teodoro de Castro (known as *Raúl*), José Humberto Bronca (known as *Zeca Fogoió*) and Guilherme Gomes Lund (known as *Luiz*). Below, from left to right: Elmo Corrêa (known as *Lourival*), Paulo Roberto Pereira Marques (known as *Amaury*), Paulo Mendes Rodrigues (known as *Paulo*) and Libero Giancarlo Castiglia (known as *Joca*). (Open source)

The annihilation of the guerrilla continued. In January 1974, Nelson Lima Piauhy Dourado, Rodolfo de Carvalho Troiano, Telma Regina Cordeiro Corrêa and Vandick Reidner Pereira Coqueiro (above), and José Lima Piauhy Dourado, Cilon da Cunha Brum, Custódio Saraiva Neto and Antônio Guilherme Ribeiro Ribas (below) were killed by the Army. (Open source)

From boxing champion, Army reserve officer and engineer graduated from the University of Prague, to guerrilla. Osvaldo Orlando da Costa (known as *Osvaldão*) was killed by a peasant, Arlindo Viera, who was acting as a guide for an Army patrol in February 1974. (Open source)

life. FAB UH-1D helicopters flew over the jungles with loudspeakers playing messages offering surrender to the guerrillas; whoever accepted was murdered.

In February 1974, the guerrilla *Osvaldão* was killed by a peasant called Arlindo Viera, also known as *Piauí*, who was leading a patrol of soldiers as a guide. The subversive was beheaded and his body transported through the forest, hanging by his legs from a rope tied to a helicopter. *Piauí* received a portion of land as a gift from the Army and lived off his fame, but he died in poverty in 1993 and his burial was paid for by the government.

By March 1974, only about 20 guerrillas still survived in the jungle, hungry, sick, with obsolete weapons, very low morale and without the logistical support of the population. Above all, they had the Army on their heels. During that month, the guerrillas Luiz René Silveira e Silva, Mara Célia Corrêa, Antônio de Pádua Costa, José Humberto Bronca, Hélio Luiz Magalhães Navarro and Demerval da Silva Pereira were all killed.

Pedro Alexandrino Oliveira Filho (known as *Peri*), found alone in the forest, was shot in the head and transported to the Xambioá base, where his body was kicked by soldiers until an officer intervened demanding respect to a dead enemy. Dinaelza Coqueiro, known as *Maria Dina*, was arrested after being denounced by peasants and taken to Captain *Curió*. She spat in his face and was shot dead. On 21 April 1974, three guerrillas – Beto, Antônio Alfaiate and *Valdir* – asked a farmer for salt and food. Unarmed, within minutes they were taken prisoner by an Army combat group that surrounded the farmhouse. A FAB UH-1D took them to Bacada and they were never seen again, certainly being eliminated. CENIMAR also recorded the death of the guerrilla Uirassu de Assis Batista (known as *Valdir*) in April 1974.

In June, Áurea Elisa Pereira Valadão (known as *Elisa*), Luíza Agusta Garlippe (known as *Tuca*) and Daniel Ribeiro Callado (known as *Doca*) were eliminated after being captured. Several others, according to witness testimony, were arrested and executed. The only foreigner in the guerrilla movement, the Italian Líbero Giancarlo Castiglia (known as *Joca*), was killed in the jungle by an Army combat group. The feared *Dina* was arrested in August 1974 along with Luíza Garlippe, a São Paulo nurse and medical commander of what remained of the guerrilla; both were executed. Suely Yomiko Kamayana, known as *Chica*, was also killed in August. The two surviving Petit brothers disappeared. Antônio de Pádua Costa, known as *Piauí*, a former astronomy student at the Department of Physics at the UFRJ who had taken command of the main guerrilla detachment after Grabois' death, was arrested after a fight in the woods with Sergeant José Vargas Jiménez, known as *Chico Dólar*, and handed over alive to the CIEX, but was never seen again, joining the ranks of the missing.

The Army's small patrols of hunters were known as Zebra Groups. They were made up of peasants and soldiers, especially sergeants and corporals, who entered the jungle for several months to hunt down the stray surviving guerrillas. Several subversives were thus killed and financial rewards paid. To identify dead guerrillas, the military photographed them before burying them in the jungle. More than 40 were photographed. When a camera was not available, the right thumb, the corpse's entire hand or even the head was cut off. In October 1974, one of the last survivors was found, barefoot and limping in the bush. This was Walkíria Afonso Costa (known as *Walk*), a former teaching student at the Federal University of Minas Geráis (UFMG). She was taken to Xambioá and executed on 25 October 1974. José Maurílio Patrício (known as *Manoel*) suffered the same fate.

Documents found years later, contained in the archive of the Chamber of Deputies and released for public consultation, show detailed orders from naval officers, one of them from the General Commander of the Marine Corps, Vice Admiral Edmundo Drummond Bittencourt in September 1972 for the elimination of captured guerrillas. In 2009, Major Curió revealed that the Brazilian Armed Forces executed 41 guerrillas in Araguaia after being arrested alive.

By March 1974, the guerrillas Luiz René Silveira e Silva, Mara Célia Corrêa, Antônio de Pádua Costa, Hélio Luiz Magalhães Navarro, Demerval da Silva Pereira and Pedro Alexandrino Oliveira Filho had been killed. (Open source)

Four more subversives were eliminated in April 1974: Dinaelza Coqueiro, Lúcio Petit da Silva, Antonio Ferreira Pinto and Uirassu de Assis Batista. (Open source)

The guerrillas Áurea Elisa Pereira Valadão (known as *Elisa*), Luíza Agusta Garlippe (known as *Tuca*), Daniel Ribeiro Callado (known as *Doca*), Dinalva Oliveira (known as *Dina*) and Suely Yomiko Kamayana (known as *Chica*) were killed in June 1974. In October of that year, Walkíria Afonso Costa (known as *Walk*) and José Maurílio Patrício (known as *Manoel*) suffered the same fate. (Open source)

Of all the guerrilla members who fought in Araguaia at the beginning of Operation Marajoara, only two escaped: Ângelo Arroyo, killed two years later in São Paulo, and Micheas Gomes de Almeida (known as *Zezinho do Araguaia*), who, accompanying Arroyo as he crossed the states of Maranhão and Ceará to escape the conflict, disappeared for more than 20 years, being found in Goiânia in 1996 after living in São Paulo under another identity. He was still alive at the time of writing.

Operation Marajoara proved highly effective, with a total of 56 guerrillas eliminated and some 200 peasants captured under suspicion of having been part of the logistical chain supporting the insurgents. The estimated death toll among the military is 16, although that is only an approximation as official sources were never made public.

Aerial Missions during Operation Marajoara

While flying at 6,000ft in the Araguaia River region, a FAB Cessna L-19E received the following radio transmission: 'Capivara 1 to Paquera 2: I inform you that there has been a wallow, over!!!' 'Capivara 1' was the codename of one of the Army platoons on a mission in the jungle that was in radio contact with the L-19E pilot. A *capivara* (capybara) is a rodent native to the region. 'Paquera 2' was the codename for the L-19E, while 'wallow' meant that there was a confrontation with the guerrillas.

As the eight aircraft of the FAB's 1° EMRA Squadron deployed to Araguaia could not use visible military serials, it was agreed to simply name the L-19Es as Paquera (Flirt) and the UH-1Hs as Sapão (Sappanwood). Thus, they received the code Paquera 1, 2, 3, and 4 and Sapão 1, 2, 3 and 4, with the missions carried out being recorded only in the flight logbooks to calculate the hours flown by each pilot. Since the region had little air traffic, and flight controllers at Marabá airport (at the time one of the few paved runways in the region) were instructed to operate following these codes, there was no problem communicating with the tower simply using these codenames.

Xambioá airfield was a dirt runway, approximately 2,000 meters long, and was operable only in good weather under visual flight (VFR) conditions. As soon as the 1° EMRA Squadron aircraft arrived in Xambioá, the construction of infrastructure capable of keeping the aircraft in flying condition began. There were no hangars and

A FAB Cessna L-19E Bird Dog, intensively used during the fight against the guerrillas in Araguaia. (MUSAL)

During the fight against the guerrillas in Araguaia, veteran Douglas C-47s and DHC-5 Buffalos were employed for transporting troops and supplies. (FAB via Hélio Higuchi)

all maintenance was carried out outdoors. Even so, it was possible to maintain a high level of operability, as spare parts were supplied directly without bureaucracy by the FAB's supplies department. Fuel came by air from Marabá, transported in drums. Once brought to the theatre of operations, the drums were allowed to 'rest' for 48 hours to decant impurities. Other supplies were brought to Xambioá by twice-weekly flights carried out by C-47s or C-115s.

A FAB Bell UH-1D flying over the forest. (FAB)

The strategy of Operation Marajoara was to confront the guerrillas by sending at least 20 small, well-equipped detachments into the forests. Each detachment was made up of approximately eight men and was guided by a peasant who knew the region very well. The missions lasted four days. They were transported by FAB UH-1H helicopters and maintained contact at least twice a day by radio with the Cessna L-19E that flew over the region at pre-established times.

Thanks to the information collected during Operation Anaconda, the approximate number of the enemy forces was known, as well as the quality of their weapons. Even so, during the early months of Operation Marajoara, combat detachments tended to be transported and disembarked using two UH-1Hs at a time, one of which, armed with two Browning .30 machine guns operated by flight mechanics, offered protection by circling the area, while the other helicopter landed the combat group in the clearings. Over time, this procedure became unnecessary and the UH-1Hs began to fly without escort. On some occasions, the UH-1Hs were armed with 70mm SBAT 70 rocket pods, which were fired to saturate areas of the forest that were believed to be harbouring guerrillas.

The main mission of the L-19E was to maintain contact in the morning and afternoon with the platoons in the forests. They always flew between 6,000 and 8,000 feet, as this altitude provided good reception for FM radio communication with patrols on the ground. They usually flew with just one crew member, who operated the radio to communicate with the platoons. The L-19Es were also equipped with rails under their wings for launching 37mm SBAT 37 rockets.

The FAB's 1° EMRA Squadron brought these rockets to Xambioá for possible use, but there was no need to use them during the campaign. In March 1973, the L-19Es were also used for psychological warfare missions against the guerrillas, for which purpose a loudspeaker was affixed under each wing on the launch rails of the SBAT 37 rockets. The pilot, when flying over the region, activated a tape previously recorded by the intelligence service in an attempt to persuade the insurgents to surrender. However, this was a trap because those who turned themselves in, after exhaustive interrogation, usually involving torture, were executed.

By January 1975, when the guerrilla movement was declared extinct, each pilot of the FAB's 1° EMRA Squadron based in Xambioá had flown more than 300 hours of combat missions. Even operating far from Belém, they did not suffer any incidents, and during the entire operation, which lasted more than a year, no serious accidents were recorded. The only accident was with a UH-1H that lost power when taking off and had to make a forced landing on some empty fuel drums. It was recovered and returned to operation within a few days.

Once the subversives were completely eradicated, the 1° EMRA's planes returned to their base in Belém do Pará, where they once again received their military serials and markings. Despite the direct participation of so few aircraft, they once again proved to be an essential element for combat in such an environment.

Operação Limpeza (Operation Cleanup)

At the beginning of 1975, with the guerrilla movement exterminated, the Brazilian Armed Forces launched an operation to conceal all the events that had taken place in Araguaia, under the policy of absolute secrecy that had been determined by the government under General Ernesto Geisel. The objective of Operation Cleanup was to erase any traces of the fighting and the bodies left behind and buried in the jungle. Approximately 68 guerrillas had been killed, around two-thirds of them having been murdered after capture and torture.

The Serra das Andorinhas (Andorinhas Mountain Range), which also became known as the Serra dos Martírios (Martyrdoms Mountain Range). (Vilma Pinheiro)

Documents were burned and camps were dismantled. During this operation, two FAB UH-1s with overpainted serial numbers and markings, with crews in civilian clothing, had the task of locating the bodies of the guerrillas buried in the jungle. Once traced, they were dug up and placed in black plastic bags, which were then taken to the Serra das Andorinhas (Andorinhas Mountain Range), which also became known as the Serra dos Martírios (Martyrdoms Mountain Range). Once there, the remains of the guerrillas were soaked in gasoline and burned in order to erase all evidence. The operation lasted around 10 days. Because of the smell of decomposition, pilots and crew members wore gas masks and perfume-soaked handkerchiefs. Reports also indicate the transport by boat of bags containing remains to the region known as 'flammable', the deepest part of the Tocantins River, near Marabá, where a similar procedure was followed to dispose of them. Once the fight against the guerrilla insurgency was over and the subsequent disposal of the bodies of the subversives was completed, all the military personnel involved swore a pact of silence.

In the following years, numerous records were made of successive concealment operations in the region, and testimonies were given by many peasants who knew the guerrillas and had a habit of being unable to keep a secret. Even many years later, during the initial period of re-democratisation in the country, there are records of similar activities being carried out by soldiers disguised as relatives, still removing bones from certain locations and dissolving them in acid, burying fragments in other places or washing them away in the rivers of the region.

General Ernesto Geisel was the only president to speak on behalf of the Brazilian government, albeit superficially, on the matter. In a message delivered to Congress on 15 March 1975, he said that there had been attempts to organise guerrilla bases in Xambioá and Marabá, north of Goiás and southeast of Pará, in undefended and distant territories, but that all had been completely defeated.[7] Unsurprisingly, the PCdoB did not accept what Geisel said, issuing a communiqué in response stating that the armed struggle against the fascist dictatorship would continue.

Ângelo Arroyo (known as *Joaquín* or *Jota*), who was eagerly sought by state security forces, managed to hide, protected by his PCdoB comrades. While in hiding, he began to plan a new guerrilla movement, travelling by bus and boat to several states to find an ideal place for a fresh insurgency. Eventually, however, Ângelo Arroyo

FAB UH-1H helicopters were used during Operation Cleanup to transport the remains of the guerrillas to the Andorinhas Mountains. (Open source)

General Ernesto Geisel was the only President of Brazil who spoke, although superficially, about the fight to eradicate the guerrilla movement on 15 March 1975 in a message to the National Congress. (Open source)

In 2014, 76-year-old retired Colonel Paulo Malhães made surprising revelations to the press about the state actions against the guerrillas in Araguaia some 40 years earlier. That same year, he was murdered in his home in Rio de Janeiro. (*Folhapress*)

The persecution of the surviving guerrillas from Araguaia continued. Ângelo Arroyo (known as *Joaquín* or *Jota*, above left) and Pedro Pomar (known as *Mário*, below left) were ambushed by the police in a house in Lapa, Rio de Janeiro, on 16 December 1976. Both resisted and were killed. (*Polícia Federal*)

and an accomplice, Pedro Pomar (known as *Mario*), were killed by a DOI-CODI team in a house in Lapa, Rio de Janeiro, on 16 December 1976. Other leaders of the PCdoB were also captured and eliminated.

The Brazilian population largely knew little or nothing about the actions of the guerrillas in the years following the fighting in Araguaia. The government imposed a code of silence and the press published almost nothing about it. Only some relatives of the subversives knew their fate, not from official sources but from some of the prisoners who survived. The inhabitants of the towns near the fighting in Araguaia did not speak publicly about the events for years, in fear of reprisals from the military. Furthermore, many of the survivors of the insurgency distanced themselves from militancy in the PCdoB.

When the country's last military government was coming to an end, many files about the fight against the guerrilla were burned, so that there would be no evidence that could in future be used against the forces of law and order.

Thereafter, a commission was installed in Congress to look into the matter, but this did not reach any conclusions, and officially at least, the military never broke its vow of silence about the combat in Araguaia. Nevertheless, there have been a few officers of the Brazilian Armed Forces who have, individually, commented on their experiences fighting the guerrilla to the press, and some of them have published books, but of course without official backing.

In 2014, retired Colonel Paulo Malhães, one of the main officers in the repression of subversives at the time – a member of CIEX and also involved in the murders and disappearances at *Casa da Morte* (the House of Death), a clandestine torture centre of the Army in Petrópolis, and in the disappearance of Federal Deputy Rubens Paiva in 1971 – gave his testimony to the National Truth Commission to clarify some of the methods used by the military against the guerrillas in Araguaia. In the second half of the 1970s, Malhães had led a 'cleaning' mission in the area disposing of the bodies of slaughtered guerrillas. They were unearthed, had their fingers and dental arches removed to prevent identification, and were thrown into rivers around the region in waterproof plastic bags filled with stones to prevent them from floating to the surface. Malhães declared that the methods used in Araguaia to dispose of the bodies were the same as those used following guerrilla deaths in urban areas. Curiously, this retired officer was found dead in unclear circumstances that same year, after his revelations were reported in the press. Was it revenge by leftist groups or a 'deletion' of files by supporters of the old repressive regime?

2
THE AFTERMATH

President General João Batista De Oliveira Figueiredo, the last military head of state in Brazil. (Open Source)

Long a taboo subject in Brazil, especially among the military, the facts related to the guerrilla movement were for many years shrouded in a veil of silence. Several books have been written about the Araguaia Guerrilla, some by former guerrillas, others by historians and even some military personnel, but these were never endorsed by government sources. Consequently, the official version of the conflict involving the Brazilian Armed Forces and the old military regimes is still unknown. Some authors have had access to official documents that have been unearthed, but the military have never publicly commented on them.

One of the most critical issues for the military and police personnel under a democratic civil government was their possible prosecution due to violations of human rights, However, the nation's last military leader, President General Figueiredo, had promulgated the Amnesty Law Nr. 6683 in August 1979, which not only included the politicians and subversives of the Left but also the torturers and repression forces of the government in the period from 2 September 1961 to 15 August 1979. For better or for worse, the Brazilian Armed Forces' 'excesses' were apparently put beyond the reach of justice. Compared to the military regimes of Argentina and Chile, Brazil's de facto governments caused few deaths. For example, actions by the Argentine regimes resulted in one death for every 2,600 people, while in Brazil there was just one death for every 280,000 people.[8]

In later years, even before the end of Brazil's military regimes, relatives and human rights organisations began the search for the missing. As early as 1980, family members of the dead travelled to the Araguaia region in search of information. In 1982, during General João Batista Figueiredo's government, 22 relatives of guerrillas filed a lawsuit against the State, asking the court to demand from the Army documents proving the deaths so that death certificates could be provided. However, on 27 March 1989, after the replacement of the judge in charge of the case, the Araguaia Guerrilla lawsuit was dismissed without any ruling on its merits, it being considered legally and physically impossible to comply with the request for the documentation. Furthermore, the judge considered that what the plaintiffs requested was covered by the Amnesty Law and did not require judicial action.

President Luiz Inácio Lula da Silva in 2003. (Agencia Brasil)

In 1991, relatives began their own excavations at the cemetery in Xambioá, which resulted in 1996 in the discovery and subsequent identification of the bones of guerrilla fighter Lúcia Petit, the first guerrilla skeleton identified by DNA. The appellants appealed the dismissal decision until 17 August 1993, obtaining a ruling from the Federal Court of Appeals, which revoked the initial decision and returned the case to the same judge to determine the facts and rule on its merits. On 24 March 1994, the Federal Government presented requests for clarification against the ruling of the Federal Chamber. The appeal was not heard by the court, based on a unanimous decision of the Court of Appeals itself on 12 March 1996. The Government filed an extraordinary appeal against this decision, which was also declared inadmissible by the Court of Appeals.

In 1995, after two decades of official silence, family members, through the international organisations Human Rights Watch and the Center for Justice and International Law (CEJIL), sent a petition to the Inter-American Court of Human Rights of the Organization of American States (OAS), for intervention with the Brazilian government for the right to information.

On 6 March 2001, the complainants appealed to the Inter-American Commission on Human Rights (IACHR), which decided to declare the case of the Araguaia Guerrilla inadmissible in relation to alleged violations of the American Declaration and the American Convention.

In July 2003, the 1st Federal Court of the Federal District ordered the breaking of confidentiality of military information about the Araguaia Guerrilla, giving the State a period of 120 days to be informed where the mortal remains of the guerrilla fighters were buried, as well as rigorous investigation within the Brazilian Armed Forces. In August of that year, the Federal Attorney General's Office appealed the ruling ordering the opening of the files, although it recognised the authors' right to try to locate the remains of their missing family members. The government of Luiz Inácio Lula da Silva created an interministerial commission on 3 October to locate remains. This committee requested the documents, but was informed that they did not exist. After passing through the Superior Court of Justice and the Federal Supreme Court, the case returned to the Court of First Instance for the sentence enforcement phase. At the time of writing, the case is still under consideration by Federal Judge Solange Salgado.

Meanwhile, in 2009, the remains of guerrilla Bergson Gurjão Farias, killed in 1972 during the first phase of operations, were identified. Together with the ones belonging to María Lúcia Petit, these are the only two cases to date of bone recovery and positive identification. In April 2009, the IACHR, a body of the OAS that oversees the observance of human rights in countries belonging to the organisation, opened a lawsuit against the Brazilian government for the arbitrary detention, torture and disappearance of 70 people, including guerrillas, local residents and peasants linked to the Araguaia Guerrilla during the Brazilian military regimes.

On 20 and 21 May 2010, the case was heard at the Inter-American Court of Human Rights. It was not until 14 December 2010 that the court ruled that Brazil violated the American Convention on Human Rights by using its Amnesty Law as a pretext for not punishing human rights violators during the military regime. In December 2010, the court accepted the IACHR's complaint and condemned the Brazilian State for using the Amnesty Law as a reason for not prosecuting the officers involved in the repression of the guerrillas.

After re-democratisation in Brazil, victims' relatives and human rights organisations began to pressure successive governments and the courts for information about the missing guerrillas and the location of their remains. In August 2011, under conditions of utmost secrecy, the FAB organised *Operação Marabá* (Operation Marabá), the first government military mission to where the crematorium of the missing guerrillas was thought to be located, at Serra das Andorinhas in the state of Pará. The expedition included representatives from the FAB, Ministry of Justice, Ministry of Defence, Special Secretariat for Human Rights and Federal Police. The soldiers were guided by retired Air Force Colonel Pedro Corrêa dos Santos Cabral, author of the book *Xambioá – Guerrilha do Araguaia*, in which he gave eyewitness details of the transportation and burning of some guerrilla remains, since he was a FAB helicopter pilot at that time. The aim was to discover the exact place where the bodies were burned and bones buried, but at the time of writing the full content of the expedition's final report is not yet known.

The only remains found and identified so far are those of Bergson Gurjão Farias (left) and María Lúcia Petit (right). (Open source)

Eight of the 17 survivors of the guerrilla adventure. Above, from left to right, Crimeia Schmidt de Almeida, Glênio Fernandes de Sá, José Genoíno Neto and Lúzia Reis Ribeiro, still young in the 1970s. Below, left to right, the veteran guerrillas João Amazonas de Souza, Elza de Lima Monnerat, Danilo Carneiro and Dagoberto Alves da Costa in the 2000s. (Open source)

Retired FAB aviator Colonel Pedro Corrêa Cabral, who published the book *Xambioá – Guerrilha do Araguaia*, a novel based on real events. (Jornal Opção)

The creation of the National Truth Commission on 16 May 2012, to investigate human rights violations that occurred in Brazil between 1946 and 1988 by agents of the State, is yet another attempt to clarify the facts relating to guerrilla warfare and to obtain documents and statements that could lead to the location of the missing in Araguaia. It is even planned to obtain foreign technological assistance for

From left to right, former Presidents of Brazil, retired generals Emílio Garrastazú Médici, Ernesto Geisel and João Baptista Figueiredo, justified the fight against the guerrilla movement. On the right, General Dilermardo Gomes Monteiro, who spoke of purification in the Army. (Open source)

DNA tests on the bones that have been found in the region over the years but have not yet been identified due to the advanced state of their degradation. The Araguaia Working Group (GTA), a body created by the Brazilian government in 2011, involves several public bodies with the mission of coordinating and executing, in accordance with appropriate scientific methodology standards, the activities necessary for the location, collection and systematisation of all the existing information and identification of the bodies of people killed in the Araguaia Guerrilla. The GTA also carries out searches and excavations in the area. Initially, the deadline for its investigations was set for 6 May 2014, but this was extended and the searches continued throughout 2015. In May 2016, at the end of President Dilma Roussef's government, the GTA was still active.

In 2016, after Michel Temer assumed the Presidency of the Republic, GTA work was halted in Araguaia. In 2016 and 2017, no expeditions were carried out in the region. According to the Federal Government at the time, this was due to changes in the government structure following the extinction and subsequent recreation of the Ministry of Human Rights, both determined by President Temer. Searches in Araguaia were carried out annually, almost always in the second half of the year (after the rainy season in the Amazon), but in 2016 and 2017 none were carried out. The period coincided with the impeachment of President Dilma Roussef and the coming to power of President Temer. There have been no new expeditions since that time, officially for bureaucratic reasons. After President Jair Bolsonaro took office, the polls were suspended by order of the new government in September 2019. Only time will tell whether the current Luíz Inácio Lula da Silva government will restart the investigations.

Epilogue

The full, detailed story of armed resistance to military regimes in Brazil may never be told. There are many reasons for this, foremost among them that most of the subversives were killed by the state security forces and those documents that could prove the excesses committed by the armed forces have been burned or were never even produced. The human remains of the guerrillas have simply disappeared in anonymous graves in inaccessible places in the Amazon jungle, although the identities of the guerrillas have been discovered thanks to investigations by the justice system and civil organisations, without the support, of course, of the Brazilian Armed Forces and Federal Police, perhaps because there have been very good reasons not to divulge the operations carried out against subversive forces in the early 1970s.

Unlike in Argentina, where military presidents and high-ranking officers were tried and convicted by civil justice, no senior military or police officer has faced trial in Brazil. Although judicial cases and investigations were opened in the era of democratic governments, no convictions were reached for those alleged to be involved in state terrorism. This is perhaps why very few military officers have dared to talk about the operations against the guerrillas in Brazil.

As for why the guerrilla insurgency failed in Brazil, there were many reasons. Most of the Araguaia guerrillas came from the middle and upper-middle classes of the cities, and were not accustomed to the rigors of the jungle. Although some had been in this environment years before the start of hostilities, they never adapted to the harsh life in the jungle, so there were many desertions. Malaria, poisonous insects and snakes and hunger undermined the morale of the guerrillas, who had to fight against better-armed specialist troops trained for fighting in the jungle. Another important factor was that the leftist students and professionals recruited by the guerrillas through the PCdoB lacked real knowledge of Brazilian society. Their political ideology distorted reality, proof of which is that they never gained adherents for their cause, with the exception of a few peasants.

Compared to the subversive operations in Cuba, Argentina and Uruguay, the Brazilian guerrillas struggled in terms of weapons, effectives, logistical support and tactics. The patient and long repressive operation during all the military regimes significantly affected the capacity for action of both the urban and rural guerrillas. Unlike the aforementioned countries, where the guerrilla organisations gained enough supporters, especially in the logistics chain, in the case of Brazil – as with Bolivia – they did not manage to recruit troops for the fight and very few peasants dared to collaborate in the logistics chain. The guerrillas were also often afraid to accept new members for fear of infiltrators. Ordinary people did not want to get involved for fear of government repression, but also because they were not convinced by the ideology that the guerrillas wanted to impose on the country.

The Brazilian military governments normally granted the guerrillas' demands when they kidnapped a foreign diplomat, so the subversives were obliged to release them once their demands were met. This did not happen in other countries, where kidnapped diplomats were normally executed by insurgents. When the guerrillas presented a list of their comrades whom they wanted to be released so as not to execute a kidnapped diplomat, the military government removed the most dangerous detainees from the list and replaced them with other prisoners of lower rank and danger. The guerrillas did not know how to negotiate properly and always accepted the government's counterproposals. Furthermore, the political prisoners were intimidated by the security forces to publicly declare on television that they refused to leave Brazil in ransom for kidnapped diplomats. The government also presented a humane face to the world, showing a readiness to negotiate with the guerrillas in order to save lives. The general population paid greater attention to soccer matches – both nationally and internationally – than any manifesto that the guerrillas managed to publish in the press. Indeed, there was absolute disinterest in everything related to the guerrilla movement.

Former President General Emílio Garrastazú Médici, after 10 years of leaving power, declared in a public statement: 'It was a war, after which it was possible to return peace to Brazil. I put an end to terrorism in this country. If we did not accept war, if we did not act drastically, we would still have terrorism today.'[9] For his part, former President General Ernesto Geisel stated: 'It was essential to repress. I cannot discuss whether the method of repression was adequate or not, or if it was the best that could be adopted. The fact is that the subversion ended.'[10] Another former President, General João Baptista Figueiredo, said in 1996: 'If there was torture during the military regime, it was carried out by low-ranking personnel, because I do not believe that a General would be capable of such a dirty thing, I don't accept that.'[11] The former heads of state thus justified what they had done in their respective governments. Finally, Army General Dilermando Gomes Monteiro, Commander of the Second Army, stated in 1976: 'No more Lamarcas or Agildos Baratas[12] will appear in our barracks, because our barracks are purified today.'[13]

APPENDICES

APPENDIX I: Interview with Brazilian Air Force Colonel Pedro Corrêa Cabral, veteran of the Araguaia Campaign against the guerrilla

Because it is considered of interest, an interview with Colonel Pedro Corrêa Cabral of the Brazilian Air Force, conducted by journalist Euler de França Belém for *Jornal Opção*, is reproduced below.

The Air Force Colonel told *Jornal Opção* that President General Emilio Garrastazu Médici authorized the hunt for Araguaia guerrillas and claims that information agents commanded the massacre.

Colonel Pedro Corrêa Cabral's interview was published in *Jornal Opção* in the editions from 30 November to 6 December 1997, and it anticipated the testimony that the retired Air Force officer gave to the Human Rights Commission of the Federal Chamber, in May 2001. He held Major Sebastião Curió responsible for the final massacre of the guerrillas of the Communist Party of Brazil (PCdoB). Curió gave an interview to *Jornal do Brasil*, in the edition of 31 March 2001, in which he said: ... "Although the *Guerrilha do Araguaia* is a dark page in Brazilian history, it is a page in history that cannot remain omitted, hidden. It has to be told. I don't see any point in hiding it..." The retired Army officer admitted that he spent four years in the guerrilla scene. Regarding the dead, he stressed: ... "In combat in the jungle, you have no way of locating bodies or transporting bodies. The most you can do is bury victims..." The Army does not want to comment on the guerrillas. The former head of the Army Social Communication Center (Ccomcex), Luiz Cesário da Silveira Filho, told *Jornal do Brasil* that the Araguaia Guerrilla is a ... "recent fact and cannot yet be considered history" ... Without a doubt, a new theory.

It is pure *cliché* to say that a work about a certain author or subject is definitive. On the history of the Brazilian left post-1964, for example, there are important but incomplete books: Jacob Gorender's *Combate nas Trevas* (*Dark Combat*), Luís Mir's *A Revolução Impossível* (*The Impossible Revolution*) and Carlos Eugênio Paz's *Viagem à Luta Armada* (*Trip to Armed Struggle*) and *Nas Trilhas da ALN"* (*On the ALN Trails*), that deserve respect, but are problematic, not in the sense that they are fake – rather, the problem is that they are too incomplete.

By opting for romanticized memoirs, the guerrillas have pseudonyms, only some are clarified at the end of the books, Carlos Eugênio clearly wrote for beginners. The other authors have problems with sources and more detailed information. The data is still being rolled out. There is a lack of more detailed information about the Left and basic information about the other side, the Right. Prejudice and, perhaps, anger have not allowed Brazilian historians and journalists to try to understand the reasons for the civil and military Right.

The collection *Os Anos de Chumbo"* (*The Years of Lead*), organized by Maria Celina D'Araújo, Gláucio Ary Dillon Soares and Celso Castro, became vital for anyone who wants to understand the military in the repressive period. The conclusion drawn is that this thinking is, in a certain way, 'crude'. But saying that doesn't clarify anything, and that is not the purpose of this presentation. One of the books in the series, *A Memória Militar Sobre a Repressão* (*The Military Memory About Repression*) has very interesting information. However, it should be noted that there is a military prejudice against almost everything that is not military.

The testimony of General Adyr Fiúza de Castro confirmed what historians have published: ... "'Corporal' Anselmo was 'turned' by Cenimar (the Navy's information service). He handed over almost everyone from PCdoB. It was his work..." He adds: ... "The instructor of the Brazilian guerrillas in Cuba was a CIA agent. He then brought and handed over to the CIEX, at the time of Miltinho (General Milton Tavares de Souza, head of the Army Information Center, CIEX), the list of all the Brazilians who went there, their performance, the codename they had. Miltinho informed us. But he received it from the CIA..." However, Fiúza did not provide the name of the informant.

Regarding the Araguaia Guerrilla (1972-1974), the generals were laconic. General Ivan de Souza Mendes opened up the most: ... "The operations in that region (of Araguaia) were being conducted by the CIEX" ... He denied that he built a bonfire to burn documents: ...

Sebastião Curió Rodrigues de Moura, former officer of the Brazilian Army at the time of the Araguaia Guerrilla. He served in the Army until 1982, retiring with the rank of Lieutenant Colonel. He then ventured into politics until his death in 2022 at the age of 87. (Open Source)

Several books were published in Brazil about the Araguaia Guerrilla and the time of military repression. (Open source)

"I didn't build a bonfire. If they burned the documents, they burned them normally. Evidently, when they were withdrawing, they were not going to leave things behind. They disposed of what they had to bring, and the rest, probably, they incinerated. But there weren't many documents, because they didn't have the means to keep files or anything like that..." He assured that he vetoed a barbecue "to celebrate the victory."

General Ivan de Souza Mendes admitted: ... "When the first actions began, the population in that region was with them..." (the PCdoB militants). And he recognized that, in the first campaigns, the Army played into the hands of an "invisible" adversary. ... "When the Army realized that it was confronting an invisible opponent, who was fleeing when very exposed, it felt that it had to change and started to fight the same war: without uniforms, without anything. He separated the population, used their anti-strategy. It was very well done. They ended up nullifying the resistance that existed..."

General José Luiz Coelho Netto guaranteed that agents were infiltrated into the PCB and PCdoB. The authors of the book asked: ... "What was the most important command to dismantle the guerrilla? ..." Coelho Netto responded: ... "The person who ended up dismantling it was Milton Tavares de Sousa, head of the CIE. Miltinho, as they called him. Good, tough, firm, intelligent. Like me, he was always considered a 'hard line'..." Regarding the most active military members of the hard line, Coelho Netto pointed to Generals Antônio Bandeira and Milton Tavares. ... "Bandeira was a great fighter, even personally. This was during the Medici period. There are the two main ones: Bandeira and Milton. There's not much more to it than that, no. In the Air Force, it was basically João Paulo Moreira Burnier..."

Historians proposed a question to General Octávio Costa: ... "As for the role of the SNI, the impression one has is that it emerged very strengthened from the first year of the Médici government" ... Costa responded: ... "It wasn't quite like that. The SNI would only be really strong with João Figueiredo and General Otávio de Medeiros. The primacy went to the Ministry of the Army, General Orlando Geisel and the CIE. The great figure of the CIE was, then, General Milton Tavares de Sousa, who later commanded the II Army. A tough, capable, intelligent man, he was the great planner of the repression actions during the time of Minister Orlando Geisel in the government of Emílio Garrastazu Médici, between 1970 and 1974. I think that much of the success of the repression was due to him, and that the SNI did not have such a prominent role ..."

Nowadays, the military still says little about the Araguaia Guerrilla. Perhaps they are not sought after with due insistence. Hence the importance of testimonies like that of retired Colonel Pedro Corrêa Cabral. He was at the scene of the Araguaia Guerrilla as an Air Force Pilot-Captain in the third and final campaign, which ended in 1974 (in 1975, the military 'cleaned' the area). He is the author of the novel *Xambioá — Guerrilha do Araguaia*" (Editora Record, 252 pages), which has already sold 12,000 copies. The Colonel lives in Alagoas at present.

Reporter: "Federal deputy José Genoino Neto, from PT (Workers Party), was one of the first guerrillas arrested. Unlike other PCdoB activists, he was spared. Why did the Armed Forces initially decide to spare the prisoners and then choose to kill and bury them in the guerrilla scene itself?"

Col. Pedro Corrêa Cabral: " The Araguaia Guerrilla had three distinct phases:

- The first was a total failure for the Armed Forces as they knew nothing about this type of combat, and there was not enough information about the opposing side.
- In the second, the Army achieved some combat success, but there were an unacceptable number of casualties, resulting in a high cost-benefit ratio, also directly due to the lack of information and incorrect combat tactics. In the two phases mentioned, in which the troops acted in accordance with the precepts of conventional warfare, the commanders were combat officers par excellence, fighting and acting as they had been taught in the military academy, that is, in accordance with the principles of ethics, time and dignity. In these two periods, if any excess occurred, the limits of the Geneva Convention were not exceeded. Thus, the arrested guerrillas were sent for trial at the competent Military Audits. A combatant would never think of executing a prisoner.
- Unfortunately, the same did not happen in the third and final phase of the Araguaia Guerrilla, characterized, above all, by the command of information agents, our 'araponga' (Araponga is a kind of bird that emits a very distinctive metallic sound), to whom all power was given. They were, so to speak, 'above good and evil', and, consequently, rules of morals, ethics, honor, or dignity were not part of the list of values of those people. Add to this context a President of the Republic who liked to pretend to be a 'good guy', smiled at the public and supported Flamengo football team, but who, behind the scenes, did not hide his 'bloodthirsty' nature. This character thought that the Araguaia prisoners would only create problems for the government and work for the Military Justice bodies. He therefore ordered the intelligence agencies to 'nip the evil in the bud', that is, to eliminate everyone, without distinction, whether in combat or out of combat, summarily, so that they would not disturb his

jingoistic government, governed by jargon from Brazil — Love it or leave it. In this way, not without the support of Brasília, information agents acted during the 3rd phase of the Araguaia Guerrilla, as reported in Xambioá."

Reporter: "Historian and journalist Luís Mir claims to have found evidence that an American general, with experience in Vietnam, participated in the Araguaia Guerrilla. According to Mir, this general was not in the guerrilla scene. He would have stayed in Manaus. His interpreter would be General Hugo Abreu. Is this a myth or is it a ruled-out possibility?"

Col. Pedro Corrêa Cabral: "I have no information to say whether journalist Luís Mir is right or not. I can, however, conjecture that such a possibility cannot be ruled out. In 1967, a few years before the events in question, when I was an intern at the 1st/4th GAV (1st Squadron of the 4th Aviation Group) in Fortaleza, I attended lectures by USAF officers who had fought in Vietnam. This is evidence that there was a close connection between the Brazilian and the U.S. Armed Forces, well before the MAP Agreement (Military Assistance Program) between Brazil and the United States was broken. However, it is worth adding that, despite the possibility of having provided assistance of this nature, the Brazilian Armed Forces were not free from the countless mistakes they made in the fight against the guerrillas. And this was due to the fact that they did not have practical knowledge about this type of conflict. This is the main reason for the failure of the first two campaigns to combat the Araguaia Guerrilla. I must add, even out of a duty of loyalty and justice, that, of all the bigwigs on the political-military scene at the time, one of those who acted with ethics and dignity, although with determination and toughness, was General Hugo Abreu. Not a single ignoble act can be attributed to him, and it is good to highlight this aspect."

Reporter: "Who was the mastermind behind the fight against the Araguaia Guerrilla, especially in the third campaign: Generals Antônio Bandeira, Hugo Abreu or Viana Moog?"

Col. Pedro Corrêa Cabral: "I can safely say that it was not General Hugo Abreu. He did not belong to the infamous intelligence community, but rather was a combatant par excellence, having trained as a paratrooper and commando. I don't have power of an attorney to defend him, and I haven't even met him in person. I am simply expressing my opinion based on what I read, what I heard from other comrades and, mainly, what I deduced from some conversations I had with Colonel Kurt Pessek, at the time he was 'deported' to Fortaleza as punishment for having been General Hugo's assistant. That said, I have no evidence to point to someone who was the mastermind behind combating the guerrillas. However, I can assure you that command of operations in Araguaia was in the hands of the head of the SNI at the time, although the most crucial decisions were submitted to the President of the Republic."

Reporter: "Who, in the Armed Forces, decided to change the entry and combat tactics in Araguaia? Who was the brain behind the campaign? Major Sebastião Curió seems more like a man of action than a creator. Is this idea valid?"

Col. Pedro Corrêa Cabral: "In the third campaign, as reported in my book, tactics and procedures, as well as food and clothing, were completely changed as a direct result of the negative teachings of the first two attempts to combat the guerrilla. Furthermore, intelligence agents discovered the PCdoB's intention to transform the region into a liberated zone, obtaining recognition from international organizations that there was a situation of internal war. In order not to allow the enemy to achieve its objective, the Armed Forces began to operate in civilian clothes, and the aircraft markings were either deleted or painted over. This made it officially more difficult to prove this situation. In this sense, it is therefore not possible to point out a central figure who would have devised this entire apparatus. The tactics and other procedures were decided in common agreement with the command bodies of each of the Single Forces, advised, respectively, by their intelligence services, CIEX, CENIMAR and CISA. Naturally, in this context, the SNI exerted great influence, since it was the central body of the system, and all guidelines regarding the search, processing and production of information emanated from it."

Brazilian Army Major General Hugo de Andrade Abreu. (EB)

"Then Major Sebastião Moura, known as Curió, was a minor figure, therefore leading to the idea that he acted in accordance with the orders he received. In fact, Curió never reached the rank of colonel; During the guerrilla he was promoted to lieutenant colonel and, after the conflict, he became involved in issues relating to the Serra Pelada Garimpo, leaving active service in the Army to become a federal deputy. To be promoted to colonel he would have to have taken the General Staff course, and this was not his case."

Reporter: "Who was the ideologue of Operation Aciso (social assistance to residents of the region where the Araguaia Guerrilla took place)?"

Col. Pedro Corrêa Cabral: "With regard to operation Aciso (Civic and Social Action), this is a normal operation of the Armed Forces, being capitulated in the doctrine of each of the Single Forces as an action of a secondary nature. It was not something that arose as a result of the guerrillas. Throughout my military career, I participated in several Aciso operations, a meritorious service that the Armed Forces, whenever possible, provides to the neediest populations throughout the national territory."

Reporter: "Did Colonel Kurt Pessek, General Hugo de Abreu's aide-de-camp, really participate in combat?"

Col. Pedro Corrêa Cabral: "I have no news that Kurt Pessek participated in the third campaign. It is possible that he participated in the first, or second, since he was a paratrooper, and the Airborne Brigade, based in Rio de Janeiro, was used in the initial campaigns, with disastrous results, as it was not prepared for this type of conflict."

The emblems of the intelligence centers of the three arms: CENIMAR (Navy), CIEX (Army) and CISA (Air Force). (Open source)

"There are books that point to the participation in the fight against the Araguaia Guerrilla by a Portuguese soldier, Colonel Hermes de Oliveira, who had combat experience in Africa."

"I am not aware that Colonel Hermes de Oliveira participated in the Araguaia Guerrilla. It is possible that the Portuguese Army was consulted, as it had extensive experience in irregular wars in its former African colonies. Furthermore, the Brazilian government has always maintained excellent relations with the motherland. Regarding this issue, I think that the Portuguese contribution would have been much more valuable than the American one, since the Araguaia Guerrilla bears a much greater similarity to African colonial conflicts than to the Vietnam War."

Reporter: "The mother of the guerrilla Divino Ferreira de Souza (Nunes), killed in combat, Maria Gomes dos Santos (Dona Santinha), asks if you remember the names of the people who were unearthed at the DNER in Marabá…" She adds: … "The (Army) guide Vanu carried Divino (who was injured) on his back to the military detachment. He stayed in cell 14 at the DNER in Marabá. The guide, although an assistant to the military, was also trapped. Not to run away. At night, he passed the corridor, walking slowly, and saw Divino. The next day, Divino was no longer there."

Col. Pedro Corrêa Cabral: "This is a question that has no relevance to the interview. After more than 20 years of the Guerrilha do Araguaia, I have difficulty remembering the names of the people who participated with me, the people I lived with at the time and, finally, those who, while alive, marked my performance as an aviator and officer of the Air Force. Now, how would I remember the names of people whose bodies were supposedly buried in the Blue House, an almost exclusive refuge for commanders and intelligence agents? In fact, from what I know and reported in *Xambioá*, I do not know that any guerrilla was buried in the DNER in Marabá. I perfectly understand Dona Santinha's anguish, but these are details that are beyond my responsibility. Likewise, I can neither confirm nor deny the statements made by the guide Vanu, whom I have not met, at least that I remember. I can, yes, say, with all due respect, that Vanu was just a guide, rude and uneducated, and, as such, had very restricted access to information, which is why his vision of the events of the time is hampered by his small horizon in relation to the dimensions of the theme."

Reporter: "How did the United States follow the Araguaia Guerrilla? Would the CIA have sent reports on the matter? Are there any archives on the subject in the USA?"

Col. Pedro Corrêa Cabral: "In relation to the CIA, the person who could offer something would be, precisely, the intelligence community. The American agency, without a doubt, must have reports on the subject, as it has always interfered in the political life of all nations, and Brazil was an important country for its anti-communist interests at that time. I do not believe, however, that the CIA has details regarding the fighting and the day-to-day activities of the conflict."

Reporter: "Is there accurate information on the number of soldiers and guerrillas killed in combat? Where is this information? Dominican Friar Gil Vila Nova said: … "When the Army entered the forest, it was unsuccessful. I felt sorry for the Army boys. Many were killed. Trucks came out full of dead soldiers. Then they used the Aborigines to hunt guerrillas, stopped wearing uniforms and grew beards. They started employing country people."

Col. Pedro Corrêa Cabral: "Exact information on the number of deaths on both sides certainly exists and must be kept by the Armed Forces' intelligence agencies. As for me, again, I can only conjecture. Although I don't know the exact numbers, I can say with confidence that more than a hundred guerrillas were killed or captured in the three campaigns. On the military side, I guarantee that no more than ten died. Friar Vila Nova's statement is frivolous and devoid of any logical basis, both with regard to the number of casualties among the military and in relation to the employment of Aborigines. When he says that the Armed Forces used the country people, then yes, he comes closer to the truth. The Armed Forces, in the third campaign, began to use soldiers from the region, an element acclimatized to the jungle and, therefore, more prepared to fight in that type of scenario. This detail is also reported in Xambioá."

Reporter: "The (defunct) *Coojornal*, from July 1978, says that the Suruí aborigines "were hired as scouts by the Army to help fight the guerrillas". Do you have more information about this?"

Col. Pedro Corrêa Cabral: "The aborigines were never used to fight, or to locate, guerrillas in Araguaia. *Coojornal's* statement is wrong. In the third campaign, woodsmen were used, that is, men from the region, accustomed to working in the forest, whether as rubber tappers or chestnut harvesters, or as wild animal hunters."

Reporter: "PCdoB says that the people of the Araguaia region (Pará and Tocantins, at that time Goiás) supported the guerrillas. A religious man in the region confirms this. Did the Armed Forces, to obtain information, actually have to torture the residents of the area? Was there no spontaneous collaboration?"

Col. Pedro Corrêa Cabral: "This issue involves at least three situations:

- 1st — Before the arrival of the troops, in fact, the population supported the guerrillas, or the 'Paulistas', as they were called. After all, an entire effort to gain the sympathy of the people of the towns, villages and cities had been meticulously carried out;
- 2nd — With the arrival of the troops and the demonstrations of force, such as in the Marabá 70 Maneuver, part of the population that previously supported, or was neutral, began to collaborate with the Armed Forces;
- 3rd — Finally and mainly, at the beginning of the third and final campaign, as reported in *Xambioá*, in many cases collaboration was imposed by force, torture and intimidation. Of course, there were many who collaborated spontaneously. It cannot be forgotten, and experience shows, that the poorest and most humble populations have a strong legalistic tendency, that is, they tend to obey and respect more effectively what comes from men in uniform (government representatives) than which comes from civilians, seen as their equals."

Reporter: "Dominican Gil Vila Nova said: "I think that the people fully supported the guerrillas. Only after the Army entered, many, out of fear, changed their minds, because they were arrested and tortured." Did popular support for the guerrillas scare the military?"

Col. Pedro Corrêa Cabral: "Support for the guerrillas by the population was not something open and declared. On the contrary, it was subtle and disguised. Therefore, in this context, it cannot be said that the population's support would have frightened the military."

Reporter: "Documents from a war are almost always kept. Were those from the Araguaia Guerrilla preserved? Where are they? Colonel Jarbas Passarinho often says that the information is in the "archives". Yes, but in which file?"

Col. Pedro Corrêa Cabral: "Again, I can only make conjectures. It is my opinion that documents about the Araguaia Guerrilla are preserved in the archives of intelligence agencies, kept under lock and key. Furthermore, I think that some elements of the so-called "information community" are in possession of confidential papers on the subject. Among these, Bullfinch must be one of them."

Reporter: "Major Curió says he has a report on the Araguaia Guerrilla at his house. Was this report produced by the Army or exclusively by Curió?"

Col. Pedro Corrêa Cabral: "The question should be directed to Bullfinch himself. How could I know? After the Araguaia Guerrilla, I never spoke to him again. At the time of publication of *Xambioá*, he said, in a letter to *Veja* magazine, that he was going to sue me. To this day I am still waiting for the court to be summoned."

Reporter: "Did an officer like Sebastião Curió have an overview of the guerrilla and privileged information from the command? What was your degree of freedom to act?"

Col. Pedro Corrêa Cabral: "Curió was a Major and only a qualified intelligence agent. He undoubtedly possessed some privileged information. Now, regarding the general vision of the war as a whole, within the scope of the Araguaia Guerrilla, I think that he not only had this vision but also greatly influenced the command in the tactical and strategic decisions to be made."

Reporter: "In addition to Curió, which other soldiers played a prominent role in the fight against the guerrillas?"

Col. Pedro Corrêa Cabral: "The number of officers, both combatants and the intelligence sector, was very large. Right away, I wouldn't be able to name them one by one. In this sense, therefore, if you named some and left out others, you would be committing injustice. It should also be added that, as I announced in the Author's Note, in *Xambioá*, it is no longer time to look for culprits and name names. Regrettable, some will say. Regrettable, I say, because although the vast majority of those soldiers in the intelligence community are, today, out of active service, there are still some who are on active duty and in the process of being promoted to the general ranks. In fact, at least one of them is already a general officer. Of course, I'm talking about my corporation, the Ministry of Aeronautics and the Brazilian Air Force. I don't know those from the other forces, Army and Navy, since, during the guerrilla war, they all used code names."

Reporter: "President Ernesto Geisel says (in a book published posthumously by Fundação Getúlio Vargas) that, when his government began, the Araguaia Guerrilla was entirely liquidated. However, his brother, General Orlando Geisel, Minister of the Medici Army, gave full support to the fight against the guerrillas. But the person leading it, from a distance, was General Milton Tavares. Can you explain, in detail, what the leadership chain was like?"

Col. Pedro Corrêa Cabral: "It is only worth remembering that today's Colonel Pedro Corrêa Cabral was, at the time, a simple aviator Captain. I knew and still know everything about the Araguaia Guerrilla, regarding the third campaign, within the theater of war. I cannot say anything about who was pulling the strings in Brasília and what the chain of command was, otherwise I would deceive you and myself by giving inconsequential 'kicks'"

Reporter: "PCdoB says that Baleia (Valkiria, owner of a bar), now deceased, was a collaborator of the military. You present her, in the novel *Xambioá*, as a collaborator of the guerrillas. Where is the truth? My impression is that you present it in an ambiguous way."

Col. Pedro Corrêa Cabral: "In fact, I purposely present the late Iraci, the Whale, in an ambiguous way, as she was truly an ambiguous figure. I knew her for a long time, but I don't know, to this day, which side she played for. As an opinion, I would venture to say that the Whale gave the impression of playing a double game, out of pure convenience, but she was neither on one side nor the other. Her party was herself. It is even possible that she was not a collaborator on either side, but merely assumed the mysterious aura of informant as a way of gaining prestige in tiny Xambioá."

Reporter: "Radio Tirana remains a mystery about which PCdoB itself remains a mystery to this day. After you wrote the book, did you get more information about her?"

Col. Pedro Corrêa Cabral: "Radio Tirana itself involves no mystery. I got tired of listening to its news in Portuguese, with fresh news about the southern region of Pará. What is mysterious is the informant, or informants, from Tirana. Nothing was ever discovered about how the information reached Albania. If PCdoB doesn't know, we, the military, know much less."

Reporter: "Which Brazilian soldiers do you admire?"

Col. Pedro Corrêa Cabral: "I admire General Luiz Alves de Lima e Silva, Marshal Eduardo Gomes, Marshal Castello Branco, Lieutenant Brigadier Lélio Lobo and some other soldiers with whom I serviced, but whose names do not resonate, among them, my classmate, already deceased, Miguel Ferreira Rodrigues de Lima, whom I mention in *Xambioá*, as well as the current commander of the 6th Regional Air Command, based in Brasília, Air Brigadier Major Henrique Marini de Souza."

Reporter: "The Armed Forces are corporatist anywhere in the world. They are closed. Disagreements are generally not exposed publicly. But the fact is that, in the Brazilian case, although the positions are not explicit, many officers were against torture and violence. Did you feel this when you were an active soldier? Did you notice this at an officer level? Did you witness any debate?"

Col. Pedro Corrêa Cabral: "In the Brazilian Air Force, a corporation for which I can answer, as I served there, trained and worked there for more than 30 years, the vast majority of officers were always against torture, seen as an act of cowardice. However, in the dark period of the military dictatorship, subjects of this nature were not discussed, spoken or even mentioned. Criticism remained repressed in everyone's chest, because in every environment, whether officers or soldiers, there was always an information agent ready to report anything he heard. I, in particular, was a bit of a rebel and, from time to time, I spoke a little more than was recommended. I carried within me the terrible memories of the guerrilla. I remember, for example, that as a Major, serving at the Officer Improvement School (EAOAr), I argued against the nomination of General João Figueiredo for President of the Republic, even going to Rio de Janeiro and looking for General Euler Bentes, opposition candidate, to pledge solidarity with him. At the time, another Major, more senior than me, told me bluntly that they had already informed CISA of my position. As a result, I was not promoted to lieutenant colonel because of merit, but because of seniority."

Reporter: "Was there dissension in the Armed Forces about the Araguaia Guerrilla, about the violence used? Was there a certain loss of control on the part of the commanders? If there was, was it intentional?"

Col. Pedro Corrêa Cabral: "With regard to the Araguaia Guerrilla, there was no dissension because decisions and actions on the subject were compartmentalized. That is, military units that were not involved in the operations were not aware of what was happening. For example, when I served in Fortaleza (CE), before being transferred to the 1st EMRA (Mixed Reconnaissance and Attack Squadron) in Belém (PA), I knew nothing about the guerrilla; I didn't even know that there were guerrillas in the south of Pará. I only found out after I arrived in Belém and, even then, I didn't know everything. I only gained knowledge about the violence used there, in the theater of maneuvers, in Xambioá and Marabá. To give you an idea, the officers of the 1st Air Transport Squadron (1st ETA), based at the same Belém Air Base, had no knowledge of what was happening in the conflict area. And, amazingly, even today there are officers from that time who know nothing about the guerrillas. These are soldiers who served in units that had no involvement in this type of problem and, therefore, were never informed about anything that was happening. Want an example? Ask Brigadier Major Reginaldo, general director of the Aerospace Technical Center (CTA), in São José dos Campos (SP), about the Araguaia Guerrilla, and he will tell you that he knows nothing. This

FAB First Mixed Reconnaissance and Attack Squadron (1o. EMRA) based at Belem AFB used armed North American T-6D Texan and Cessna O-1 Bird Dogs in the 1970s. (Courtesy of Albert Grandolini)

FAB First Air Transport Squadron (1o. ETA) located at Belem AFB used PBY-5A Catalina and C-47s in the 1970s. (FAB via Hélio Higuchi)

and many other officers were, and still are, involved in the technology area and never knew anything. You will say: but these are justified by their activities. Then ask the same question to an officer who, at that time, was serving in the 1st Fighter Group, in Santa Cruz (RJ). This one, too, will not know how to answer anything. When you talk about loss of control on the part of commanders regarding violence, I think you are referring to violence perpetrated by the intelligence community. If so, I respond that, in a certain way, the statement is true. The monster was created and then control over it was lost."

Reporter: "Why was the order to kill, and not arrest the guerrillas?"

Col. Pedro Corrêa Cabral: "The allegation that the intelligence personnel presented, with the greatest poker face in the world, was that, if the prisoners were kept alive, they would create a series of legal problems in the future; problems that would only bring annoyance to the revolutionary government; therefore — "it's better to eliminate evil at the root, believe me, João Pedro" — a member of information told me, at that time, and who, today, as a colonel, is in line to be promoted to brigadier."

Reporter: "In the book *Xambioá*, you tell the story of guerrillas who surrendered, collaborated with the military, but were coldly murdered. Were there many cases? Could you tell me the names of the dead? In your book, the names are fictitious."

Col. Pedro Corrêa Cabral: "This question is answered, in part, in *Xambioá* itself. There weren't many cases, but if it were just one, it

Bell UH-1H serial FAB-8554. (Courtesy of Albert Grandolini)

would be enough to vehemently abhor. Unfortunately, I am unable to give you names. Memory could betray me. I dare say, based on the photographic faces, that two of those sacrificed, after being taken prisoner, were probably Sônia Moroni and Dina. Regarding this, a companion of mine who served in Araguaia, Colonel Delamora, talking to me at the launch of the book in Rio de Janeiro, recalled with precision that Dina had been trapped in Casa Azul before "travelling". However, although I trust Delamora a lot, I'm not completely sure. I saw, it is true, several prisoners who later "travelled". At the time, I knew their names, but, unfortunately, it didn't occur to me to write them down and, today, I no longer remember them."

Reporter: "Who really was the pregnant guerrilla? "

Col. Pedro Corrêa Cabral: "Possibly Dina or Sônia Moroni. I am not sure."

Reporter: "What type of awards did the soldiers who participated in Araguaia receive: promotions, medals and accolades in their professional history?"

Col. Pedro Corrêa Cabral: "No record of participation in Araguaia remained. In our flight logs, the missions carried out in the guerrilla are recorded as simple local flights. No praise, no mention. Nothing."

Reporter: "What was seized from the guerrillas, besides food and some weapons? Did they seize diaries, reports, books and correspondence?"

Col. Pedro Corrêa Cabral: "I don't know that they seized books, diaries, or any other papers from the guerrillas. However, I do not rule out this possibility, although I have no idea where this material would be."

Reporter: "Did you talk to some of the arrested guerrillas? What did they say? Even in prison, did they maintain their convictions? Were they very young people? Were they very exhausted, hungry?"

Col. Pedro Corrêa Cabral: "Phew! It's a flurry of questions on the same issue. In fact, I spoke to some, on different and different occasions. They were all young, haggard, thin and with deep-set eyes. They were not hungry, as they had been fed by the soldiers themselves. Our conversation, each time, was about trivialities. It was impossible to have a more consistent dialogue regarding the guerrilla, or political matters, since there was always the presence of an information agent. Furthermore, the prisoners were constantly scared to say anything more serious. There was no time to establish greater trust with them. I was seen as the enemy."

Reporter: "Why, in the third campaign, was it so easy to destroy the Araguaia guerrillas? What went right in this campaign and what went wrong in the first two?"

Col. Pedro Corrêa Cabral: "The main factor that established the difference between the third campaign and the first two was information. The notable Sun Tzu, author *of The Art of War*, already announced, around 600 years before Christ: "First of all, know your enemy; Without knowing it, victory will not smile upon you…" This aspect is well explained in *Xambioá*, as well as other factors that contributed to the destruction of the guerrilla, all linked to operational measures and which were learned from the mistakes of the first campaigns."

Reporter: "How was the presence of the communists discovered: with the arrest of militant Pedro Albuquerque or through a spontaneous confession by militant Lúcia Regina de Souza Martins?"

Col. Pedro Corrêa Cabral: "Pedro Albuquerque, I believe, was the student arrested in Ceará by the Federal Police, around 1969 (or 1971, according to other versions), and, without a doubt, he was the key to discovering the focus of the guerrilla in the South of Pará. About the militant Lúcia Regina, I know nothing about. In fact, by the way, most of the questions you ask should be directed to someone in the intelligence community. As I mentioned before, I don't know everything and, on the contrary, I didn't have access to a lot of information for obvious reasons."

Reporter: "The story that at least one agent was infiltrated among the guerrillas is contested by PCdoB. In his novel, agent Gabriel

(Simplício) is infiltrated. Is it pure fiction or based on real events? There are suspicions, in fact, that someone from PCdoB, when arrested, collaborated with the military. Is this true? In your statement to the External Committee on Missing Politicians of the Chamber of Deputies, you record: "Some (agents) with the mission of infiltrating guerrilla groups""

Col. Pedro Corrêa Cabral: "The story of agent Gabriel, or Simplício, is based on real events. Agents were infiltrated in the phase leading up to the third campaign. Naturally, the way in which I narrated Gabriel's participation, as well as the Japanese Tanaka and other characters, was a product of my imagination. I wasn't in the forest with them, I wasn't even in Xambioá, or in Marabá, at the time of the Intelligence Operation, since this preceded the third campaign. I constructed these passages based on reports, or fragments of reports, that I heard here and there, during my stay in the region. I met the Japanese Tanaka, for example, but I exchanged few words with him. His universe was different from mine."

Reporter: "To this day, PCdoB considers João Carlos Campos Wisnesky, known as Paulo, to be a whistleblower and considers his escape to be very strange. He said he fled because the guerrillas didn't attack, they just retreated. Was he really a collaborator of the Armed Forces?"

Col. Pedro Corrêa Cabral: "I can't say anything about João Carlos Wisnesky, Paulo. I simply give an opinion that during the third campaign I did not know of any case of denunciation by guerrillas. I believe that, if there had been, I would have known about it, as the fact would have been discussed among the officers."

Reporter: "There is a story that Rosalindo de Souza, known as Mundico, was prosecuted by PCdoB in Araguaia because he wanted to escape the region. It is the version of a Colonel who served in the Army Information Center (according to *Veja* magazine). Ângelo Arroyo's report guarantees that he died while handling his gun, which he fired accidentally. Historian Romualdo Pessoa presents another version. Mundico was reportedly killed by a farmer who informed General Antônio Bandeira when he was looking for food. What do you know about this story?"

Col. Pedro Corrêa Cabral: "Likewise, I know nothing about Rosalindo de Souza. I have not read the Arroyo Report. I emphasize that I wrote *Xambioá* consulting only my memory. I did not rely on any publication on the subject. It was only after the book was released that some material came into my hands that, eventually, could have been useful in the construction of *Xambioá*. Among these, for example, I mention the publication *História Imediata: A Guerrilha do Araguaia* (*Immediate History: The Araguaia Guerrilla*), written by Palmério Dória and others. I received a copy, on 19 May 1994, with a dedication from Mário Lúcio Franco, a cousin who lives in Belo Horizonte and who is a researcher on Araguaia issues."

Reporter: "Who coordinated the operation to dig up and burn the bodies of the guerrillas?"

Col. Pedro Corrêa Cabral: "It is not a case of mentioning names. The operation was coordinated by intelligence personnel who, moreover, coordinated all other actions in the area."

Reporter: "Would you return to Serra das Andorinhas?"

Col. Pedro Corrêa Cabral: "I am ready to return to Serra das Andorinhas, whenever requested. I don't understand why so much emphasis was placed on Vanu's unfounded statements, which resulted in useless excavations in the DNER area, in Marabá (Casa Azul)."

Reporter: "How many soldiers were used to combat the Araguaia Guerrilla?"

Col. Pedro Corrêa Cabral: "I do not have the elements to provide this type of information. The number of personnel in the region varied greatly in different phases and on different occasions. Teams of fighters were replaced frequently."

Reporter: "Why didn't anyone in the Armed Forces publicly support you when you released the book?"

Col. Pedro Corrêa Cabral: "In fact, I did not receive public support from any of my colleagues in uniform. However, I received numerous phone calls and some letters of solidarity. Among these demonstrations, I quote the words of Lieutenant Brigadier Murillo Santos: ... "Pedro, the people who are speaking ill of you are speaking because they haven't read your book. They are based on the sensationalist news from *Veja* magazine. I read your book, I really liked it and I spoke to Lobo (Lieutenant-Brigadier, Minister of the Air Force) to read it and recommend it to the troops.""

Reporter: "You and historian Romualdo Pessoa (author of *Guerrilha do Araguaia — A Esquerda em Armas*) disagree on one point. You say that, after being arrested, no guerrilla left the third campaign alive. Professor Romualdo writes: "Former soldier José dos Santos Aniká, who served at the Clevelândia do Norte (AP) military base, also stated that Dina was captured and taken alive to Rio de Janeiro: 'Everyone in the Army celebrated her arrest, because she had shot an officer in the mouth with a gunshot. She was feared by everyone.'" What's true about that?"

Col. Pedro Corrêa Cabral: "I repeat: no one escaped Araguaia alive, except (Ângelo) Arroyo [Zenóbio in the novel *Xambioá*]. The aforementioned soldier's report is completely baseless."

Reporter: "Is it true that you received threats for publishing the book? What type of threat?"

Col. Pedro Corrêa Cabral: "At the time the book was released, I received numerous threats by phone and some by letter. I have these saved. There were death threats to me and my family, psychological terrorism that left us quite shaken. At the height of the problem, I stopped attending an interview at "Jô, Onze e Meia" due to an absolute lack of security. A friend of mine, Roberto Parreira, now head of vice-president Marco Maciel's office, told me: ... "Don't worry, Pedro, if they kill you, Lysia will become rich, because *Xambioá* will become the biggest best-seller of all time..." Great humor from Parreira..."

Reporter: "The memoir-novel *Xambioá — Guerrilha do Araguaia* seems unfinished, waiting for a sequel. Do you intend to write another book?"

Col. Pedro Corrêa Cabral: "I don't know if I would be willing to write about Araguaia again. I have incorporated other values in recent years, and now I have written things that have nothing to do with violence, torture, or the injustices committed in the years of lead. I accepted the absolute reign of Jesus in my life and became a new creature. My writings today concern the immense and immeasurable love of the Lord for all of us sinners. I am writing a book about the Holy Scriptures whose working title is: 'Stories of the Stories of the Bible'."

Reporter: "Has any filmmaker been interested in adapting the book to film?"

Col. Pedro Corrêa Cabral: "Regarding the project of transforming *Xambioá* into a film, I tell you that there are conversations in this regard. There are interested filmmakers, and a professional is already working on the script. I think we are in time to show Brazilians, by all means, the hidden episodes of our history."

"Initially, the left received his book with suspicion. Now, it is accepted as true. But the irritation in the Armed Forces was intense."

"I think the initial distrust of the Left is natural. However, research into the Araguaia Guerrilla is demonstrating that *Xambioá* is not only a true book, but, above all, that it was written with the soul and with the highest spirit of Brazilianness."

Reporter: "Why did you choose a kind of memoir-novel to shape your denunciation book? Did the book sell well? Did you make money? "

Col. Pedro Corrêa Cabral: "The literary form aimed to fill in the blanks of memory, especially with regard to people's names. I believe that in terms of Brazil, my book sold well, around 12,000 copies. I also believe that the release of the film will boost book sales. Did I earn money? I can't say no, but the reason I wrote *Xambioá* was never money, just idealism and the desire to get something out that bothered me a lot."

Reporter: "Were the doctors who revived tortured people from the Army?"

Col. Pedro Corrêa Cabral: "They were military. Full stop."

Reporter: "For you, what is the big question that remains to be answered about the Araguaia Guerrilla?"

Col. Pedro Corrêa Cabral: "I think this is not an issue of answering a big question, but rather of the Armed Forces removing everything about the Araguaia Guerrilla from its archives. And not only that, I always pray that other soldiers who participated in that dirty war will be willing to tell everything they know. May Bullfinch tell the truth, repent of his sins and ask God for forgiveness for the barbarities he committed."

APPENDIX V: Personnel and Casualties of the Araguaia War

TABLE 26: Senior Military Officers Involved in the Araguaia War [14]

Officer	Position
General of the Army Emílio Garrastazú Médico	President of Brazil 1969–1974
General of the Army Ernesto Geisel	President of Brazil 1974–1979
Army General João Baptista Figueiredo	SNI Chief in 1974. Later President of Brazil 1979–1985
Army General Orlando Geisel	Army Minister 1969–1974. (President Ernesto Geisel's brother)
Army General Olavo Vianna Moog	Commander of the Planalto Military Command
Army General Álvaro Cardoso	Amazónia Military Commander
Army General Antônio Bandeira	3rd Infantry Brigade Commander 1972
Army General Hugo Abreu	Araguaia Command Officer 1973
Army General Carlos Alberto Brilhante Ustra	Second Army DOI-CODI Commander 1970–1974
Army General Milton Tavares	CIEX Chief 1969–1974
Army General Nilton de Albuquerque Cerqueira	DOI-CODI Commander in Salvador 1971
Army General Sylvio Frota	Army Minister 1974–1977
Army Colonel Raúl Augusto de Mendonça Borges	Commander of the 2nd Section of the 8th Military Region 1972
Army Lieutenant Colonel Carlos Sérgio Torres	CIEX Chief of Operations in Xambioá
Army Lieutenant Colonel Arnaldo Bastos de Carvalho Braga	Chief of CIEX in Brasília DF
Army Major Gilberto Airton Zenkner	Operation Ananconda General Coordinator
Army Major Othon Rêgo Monteiro Filho	PIC-Brasília Commander 1972
Army Captain Aluísio Madruga de Moura e Souza	Based in Araguaína during Operation Anaconda
Navy Corvette Captain Uriburu Lobo da Cruz	Commander of the Marine Corps Operative Group in Araguaia
Navy Corvette Captain Hermenegildo Pereira da Silva Filho	Navy Information Command
Navy Captain-Lieutenant Eduardo Celso Rodriguez Serra	Amphibian Division of the Marines Corps

TABLE 27: Military Fatalities 1972–1974 [15]

Rank & Name	Military Unit	Place & Date
Army 3rd Sergeant Francisco das Chagas Alves Brito	2° BIS – Belém	São Domingos, Sergipe 16 October 1973
Army 2nd Sergeant Mário Abrahim da Silva	1° BIS – Manáus	Araguaia Region 28 September 1972
Army Corporal Odílio da Cruz Rosa	5° Guards Company – Belém	Araguaia Region 8 May 1972
Army Corporal Ovídio França Gomes	1°/34° Infantry Battalion – Macapá	Araguaia Region 16 February 1974
Army First Soldier Jaime Luiz Kardiwski	1° Cavalry Regiment – Brasília	Araguaia Region 25 September 1972
Army Soldier João Francisco Picanço do Nascimento	1°/34° Infantry Battalion – Macapá	Araguaia Region 28 October 1972
Army Soldier Luiz Antônio Ferreira	25° Cavalry Battalion	Araguaia Region in 1972
Army Soldier Pedro Pinto Paixão	2° BIS – Belém	Araguaia Region 21 June 1972
Army Soldier Raúl Marques de Brito	5° Guards Company – Belém	Araguaia Region 8 December 1973
Army Soldier Francisco Waldir de Paula	8° Anti-Aircraft Artillery Group – Brasília	São Geraldo, Pará 1974
Officially acknowledged casualties, but it is estimated that more military personnel died in Araguaia		

TABLE 28: Military Wounded in Combat 1972–1974[16]		
Rank & Name	Military Unit	Place & Date
Army Major Lício Augusto Ribeiro Maciel	CIEX – Military Engineer & Paratrooper	Araguaia Region October 1973
Army Captain Sebastião Rodrigues de Moura	CIEX – Operation *Anaconda* Coordinator	Araguaia Region October 1973
Army 1st Lieutenant Álvaro de Souza Pinheiro	Paratroopers Brigade – Rio de Janeiro	Araguaia Region 2 June 1972
Army 2nd Lieutenant Cláudio Roberto Pereira Cunha	2° BIS – Belém	Oito Barracas, Pará 29 September 1972
Army 3rd Sergeant Francisco Adalmir Nunes da Silva	5° Guards Company – Belém	Araguaia Region 14 March 1974
Army 3rd Sergeant Raymundo Barbosa	5° Guards Company – Belém	Pau Preto 29 May 1972
Army 3rd Sergeant Wellisbeth Moraes Macedo	5° Guards Company – Belém	Araguaia Region 8 May 1972
Army Soldier Manoel Pastana da Silva	2° BIS – Belém	Araguaia Region 1973
Army Soldier Milton Santa Brígida Ferreira	5° Guards Company – Belém	Marabá 3 June 1972
Officially acknowledged, but it is estimated that more military personnel were wounded in combat in Araguaia		

TABLE 29: Araguaia Guerrilla Members[17]				
Name	Known as	Born in (city/state/year)	Profession	Fate
Lourival de Moura Paulino	?	? in 1917	Boatman	Killed 21 May 1972
Bergson Gurjão Farias	*Jorge*	Fortaleza, Ceará in 1947	Chemistry student	Killed 2 June 1972
Idalísio Soares Aranda Filho	*Aparício*	Rubim, Minas Geráis in 1947	University student	Killed 13 June 1972
Maria Lúcia Petit da Silva	*María*	Agudos, São Paulo in 1950	School teacher	Killed 16 June 1972
Kleber Lemos da Silva	*Carlito*	Rio de Janeiro, Rio de Janeiro in 1942	Economist	Killed 29 June 1972
Miguel Pereira dos Santos	*Cazuza*	Recife, Pernambuco in 1943	Bank clerk	Killed 20 September 1972
Antônio Monteiro Teixeira	*Antônio*	Ilhéus, Bahía in 1941	Geologist	Killed 20 September 1972
José Toledo de Oliveira	*Vitor*	Uberlândia, Minas Geráis in 1941	Lawyer	Killed 21 September 1972
Helenira Resende de Souza	*Fátima*	Cerqueira César, São Paulo in 1944	University student	Killed 29 September 1972
Francisco Manoel Chaves	*Zé Francisco*	? in 1912	Former military sailor	Killed 29 September 1972
Ciro Flávio Salazar de Oliveira	*Flávio*	Araguarí, Minas Geráis in 1943	University student	Killed 30 September 1972
João Carlos Haas Sobrinho	*Dr Juca*	São Leopoldo, Rio Grande do Sul in 1941	Medical doctor	Killed 30 September 1972
Manoel José Nurchis	*Gil*	São Paulo, São Paulo in 1940	Factory worker	Killed 30 September 1972
Carlos Nicolau Danielli	*Pontes*	Niterói, Rio de Janeiro in 1929	Politician	Killed 30 December 1972
Vandick Raidner Coqueiro	*João Goiano*	Boa Nova, Bahía in 1949	School teacher	Killed 17 January 1973
Rosalindo de Sousa	*Mundico*	Itaguaçu, Bahía in 1940	Lawyer	Killed 16 August 1973

João Gualberto Calatroni	*Zebão*	Nova Venécia, Espíritu Santo in 1951	University student	Killed 13 October 1973
Divino Ferreira de Sousa	*Nunes*	Caldas Novas, Goiás in 1942	Merchant	Killed 13 October 1973
André Grabois	*Zé Carlos*	Rio de Janeiro, Rio de Janeiro in 1947	Student	Killed 14 October 1973
Antônio Alfredo de Lima	*Alfredo*	?, Pará in 1938	Peasant	Killed 14 October 1973
Lúcia Maria de Souza	*Sônia*	São Gonçalo, Rio de Janeiro in 1944	University student	Killed 24 October 1973
Jaime Petit da Silva	*Jaime*	Iacanga, São Paulo in 1945	Engineer	Killed 28 November 1973
Antônio Guilherme Ribas	*Ferreira*	São Paulo, São Paulo in 1946	University student	Killed 28 November 1973
Adriano Fonseca Filho	*Chicão*	Ponte Nova, Minas Geráis in 1945	University student	Killed 3 December 1973
José Lima Piauhy Dourado	*Ivo*	Barreiras, Bahía in 1946	Photographer	Killed 14 December 1973
Gilberto Olímpio Maria	*Pedro*	Mirassol, São Paulo in 1942	Journalist	Killed 15 December 1973
Tobias Pereira Barroso Jr.	*Jonás*	Rio de Janeiro, Rio de Janeiro in 1949	University student	Killed 17 December 1973
Maurício Grabois	*Mário*	Salvador, Bahía in 1912	Politician	Killed 25 December 1973
Líbero Giancarlo Castiglia	*Joca*	San Lucido, Cosenza, Italy in 1944	Factory worker	Killed 25 December 1973
Paulo Mendes Rodrigues	*Paulo*	Cruz Alta, Rio Grande do Sul in 1931	Economist	Killed 25 December 1973
José Humberto Bronca	*Zeca Fogoió*	Porto Alegre, Rio Grande do Sul in 1934	Factory worker	Killed 25 December 1973
Guilherme Gomes Lund	*Luis*	Rio de Janeiro, Rio de Janeiro in 1947	University student	Killed 25 December 1973
Elmo Corrêa	*Lourival*	Rio de Janeiro, Rio de Janeiro in 1946	University student	Killed 25 December 1973
Paulo Roberto Pereira Marques	*Amaury*	Pain, Minas Geráis in 1949	Bank clerk	Killed 25 December 1973
Antônio Teodoro de Castro	*Raul*	Itapipoca, Ceará in 1945	University student	Killed 25 December 1973
Luíz Vieira de Almeida	*Luizinho*	?	Peasant	Killed 1973
Pedro Matias de Oliveira	*Pedro Carretel*	?	Rural worker	Killed 2 January 1974
Nelson Piauhy Dourado	*Nelito*	Jacobina, Bahía in 1941	Public employee	Killed 2 January 1974
Jana Moroni Barroso	*Cristina*	Fortaleza, Ceará in 1948	University student	Killed 2 January 1974
Maria Célia Corrêa	*Rosa*	Rio de Janeiro, Rio de Janeiro in 1945	Bank clerk	Killed 2 January 1974
Rodolfo de Carvalho Troiano	*Manoel do A*	Juiz de Fora, Minas Geráis in 1949	University student	Killed 12 January 1974
Marcos José de Lima	*Ari Armeiro*	?	Gunsmith	Killed 12 January 1974
Antônio Ferreira Pinto	*Alfaiate*	Lagoa dos Gatos, Pernambuco in 1932	Tailor	Killed 14 January 1974
Antônio de Pádua Costa	*Piauí*	Luís Corrêia, Piauí in 1943	University student	Killed 14 January 1974
Luis René Silveira e Silva	*Duda*	Rio de Janeiro, Rio de Janeiro in 1951	University student	Killed 14 January 1974

Osvaldo Orlando da Costa	*Osvaldão*	Passa Cuatro, Minas Geráis in 1938	Mechanical engineer	Killed 4 February 1974
Custódio Saraiva Neto	*Lauro*	Fortaleza, Ceará in 1952	University student	Killed 15 February 1974
Cilon da Cunha Brum	*Simão*	São Sepé, Rio Grande do Sul in 1946	University student	Killed February 1974
Demerval da Silva Pereira	*Joao Araguaia*	Salvador, Bahía in 1945	Lawyer	Killed 28 March 1974
Dinaelza Soares Santana	*Mariadina*	Vitória da Conquista, Bahía in 1949	University student	Killed 8 April 1974
Hélio Luiz Navarro	*Edinho*	Rio de Janeiro, Rio de Janeiro in 1949	University student	Killed 14 April 1974
Lúcio Petit da Silva	*Beto*	Piratininga, São Paulo in 1943	Electronic engineer	Killed 21 April 1974
Uirassu de Assis Batista	*Valdir*	Itapicurú, Bahía in 1952	University student	Killed 29 April 1974
Batista	*?*	?	Peasant	Killed 30 April 1974
Áurea Eliza Valadão	*Elisa*	Monte Belo, Minas Geráis in 1950	University student	Killed 13 June 1974
Daniel Ribeiro Callado	*Doca*	São Gonçalo, Rio de Janeiro in 1940	Factory worker	Killed 28 June 1974
Dinalva Oliveira Teixeira	*Dina*	Castro Alves, Bahía in 1945	Geologist	Killed 16 July 1974
Luíza Augusta Garlippe	*Tuca*	Araraquara, São Paulo in 1941	Nurse	Killed 16 July 1974
Pedro Alexandrino de Oliveira	*Peri*	Belo Horizonte, Minas Geráis in 1947	Bank clerk	Killed 4 August 1974
Telma Regina Cordeiro Corrêa	*Lia*	Rio de Janeiro, Rio de Janeiro in 1947	University student	Killed 7 September 1974
José Maurílio Patrício	*Manoel do B*	Santa Teresa, Espírito Santo in 1944	University student	Killed September 1974
Suely Yumiko Kanayama	*Chica*	Coronel Macedo, São Paulo in 1948	Language teacher	Killed September 1974
Walquíria Afonso Costa	*Walk*	Uberaba, Minas Geráis in 1947	School teacher	Killed 25 October 1974
Arildo Aírton Valadão	*Ari*	Itaici, Espíritu Santo in 1948	University student	Killed 24 November 1974
Orlando Momente	*Landin*	Rio Claro, São Paulo in 1933	Factory worker	Killed 1974
Ângelo Arroyo	*Joaquim*	São Paulo, São Paulo in 1928	Union leader	Killed 16 December 1976
Pedro Ventura Pomar	*?*	Óbidos, Pará in 1913	Former politician	Killed 16 December 1976
Glênio Fernandes de Sá	*Glênio*	Caraúbas, Rio Grande do Norte in 1950	University student	Survived. Died in 1990
Dower Morães Cavalcanti	*Domingos*	Fortaleza, Ceará in 1950?	University student	Survived. Died in 1992
João Amazonas de Souza	*Velho Cid*	Belém, Pará in 1912	Factory worker	Survived. Died in 2002
Elza de Lima Monnerat	*Dona Maria*	Sapucaia, Rio de Janeiro in 1913	School teacher	Survived. Died in 2004
Danilo Carneiro	*Nilo*	Senador Firmino, MG in 1941	Engineer	Survived. Died in 2022
Micheas Gomes de Almeida	*Zezinho*	Capanema, Pará in 1934	Construction worker	Survived. Still alive
Eduardo Monteiro Texeira	?	?	Shop owner	Survived. Still alive

José Genoíno Neto	*Geraldo*	Quixeramobim, Ceará in 1946	Politician	Survived. Still alive
Lúzia Reis Ribeiro	*Lúcia*	Jequié, Bahía in 1949	University student	Survived. Still alive
Crimeia Schmidt de Almeida	*Alice*	Rio de Janeiro, Rio de Janeiro in 1948	University student	Survived. Still alive
Regilena da Silva Carvalho	*Lena*	Pedralva, Minas Geráis in 1947	Politician	Survived. Still alive
Lúcia Regina de Souza	*Regina*	São Paulo, São Paulo in 1951	University student	Survived. Still alive
Rioko Kayano	?	?	Nurse	Survived. Still alive
Pedro Albuquerque Neto	*Pedro*	Fortaleza, Ceará in 1944	University professor	Survived. Still alive
Tereza Cristina Cavalcanti	?	?	University student	Survived. Still alive
João Carlos Campos Winesky	*Paulo Paquetá*	Paquetá, Guanabara in 1943	Soccer player	Survived. Still alive
Dagoberto Alves da Costa	*Miguel*	São Luís, Maranhão in 1944	Psychologist	Survived. Still alive
Total number of guerrillas: 85. Killed: 68. Survived: 17				

NOTES

1 Manioc, commonly called cassava or yucca, is a woody shrub of the spurge family, native to South America, especially Paraguay and Brazil, extensively cultivated for its edible starchy root tuber, a major source of carbohydrates.

2 *Caboclo* is the term used in Brazil to designate mixed race, part white European and part indigenous South American.

3 *Carajá* or *Karajá* are indigenous people of the *macro-yê* linguistic family, who have lived in the Araguaia river basin for a very long time.

4 Romualdo Pessoa Campos Filho, *A Esquerda em Armas: História da Guerrilha do Araguaia (1972–1975)*. Dissertação apresentada no curso de pós-graduação do Instituto de Ciências Humanas e Letras da Universidade Federal de Goiás para o mestrado em História das Sociedades Agrárias em fevereiro de 1995 (Dissertation presented in postgraduate course at the Institute of Human Sciences and Letters of the Federal University of Goiás for a Master's degree in History of Agrarian Societies in February 1995).

5 The expression 'gringo' means a person who was born in the United States, or simply a foreigner. The term came into use during the American–Mexican War (1846–1848), when Mexican soldiers shouted 'Greens go home' – shortened to 'Gringo' – to the Americans (green because the American uniform was that colour).

6 *Marajoara*: the *Marajó* or *Marajoara* culture was a pre-Columbian civilisation that flourished on the island of Marajó, at the mouth of the Amazon River.

7 Elio Gaspari, *A Ditadura Escancarada, As Ilusões Armadas*, Vol. II (São Paulo: Cia das Letras, 2003).

8 Thomas E. Skidmore, *The Politics of Military Rule in Brazil, 1964–1985* (New York: Oxford University Press, 1988).

9 Elio Gaspari, *A Ditadura Escancarada. As Ilusões Armadas*, Vol. II (São Paulo: Cia das Letras, 2003).

10 Elio Gaspari, *A Ditadura Escancarada. As Ilusões Armadas*, Vol. II (São Paulo: Cia das Letras, 2003).

11 Elio Gaspari, *A Ditadura Escancarada. As Ilusões Armadas*, Vol. II (São Paulo: Cia das Letras, 2003).

12 Agildo da Gama Barata Ribeiro was a revolutionary military officer who joined the Revolution of 1932 and the Communist Attempt of 1935 when he was a captain in the 3rd Infantry Regiment in Praia Vermelha.

13 Celso Castro, *A Invenção do Exército Brasileiro*, Serie Descubrindo o Brasil (São Paulo: Editora Zahar, 2002).

14 Taís Morais & Eumano Silva, *Operação Araguaia. Os Arquivos Secretos da Guerrilha* (São Paulo: Geração Editorial, 2011).

15 Taís Morais & Eumano Silva, *Operação Araguaia. Os Arquivos Secretos da Guerrilha* (São Paulo: Geração Editorial, 2011).

16 Taís Morais & Eumano Silva, *Operação Araguaia. Os Arquivos Secretos da Guerrilha* (São Paulo: Geração Editorial, 2011).

17 https://pt.wikipedia.org/wiki/Lista_de_guerrilheiros_do_Araguaia.

SOURCES

Books

Amorin de Angelo, Vítor, *Luta Armada no Brasil*, Coleção Saber de Tudo (São Paulo: Editora Claridade, 2009)

Andrade, John M., *Latin-American Military Aviation*, 1st Edition (Leicester: Midland Counties Publications, 1982)

Butler, Phil & Dan Hagedorn, *Air Arsenal North America. Aircraft for the Allies 1938–1945. Purchases and Lend-Lease* (Hinckley, UK: Midland Publishing, 2004)

Cabral, Pedro Corrêa, *Xambioá – Guerrilha no Araguaia* (Rio de Janeiro: Editora Record, 1993)

Camazano Alamino, Cel. Av. (Ret.) Aparecido, *A Saga dos Guerreiros Polivalentes. Aviação de Reconhecimento e Ataque na FAB*, No. 38. (Rio de Janeiro: Instituto Histórico-Cultural da Aeronáutica/INCAER, 2015)

Camazano Alamino, Cel. Av. (Ret.) Aparecido, *Gloster Meteor. O Primero Jato do Brasil*, 1ª Edição (São Paulo: C&R Editorial, 2010)

Carvalho, Luiz Maklouf, *O Coronel Rompe o Silencio* (Rio de Janeiro: Editora Objetiva, 2004)

Castro, Celso, *A Invenção do Exército Brasileiro*, Serie Descubrindo o Brasil (São Paulo: Editora Zahar, 2002)

Corrêa Cabral, Captain (Ret.) Pedro, *Justicia e Democracia: as novas perspectivas da hermenêutica constitucional*, Vol. II (Raleigh, NC: Lulu Publishing, 2017)

Flores Jr, Jackson, *Aeronaves Militares Brasileiras 1916–2015* (Rio de Janeiro: Action Editora, 2015)

Flores Jr, Jackson, *Aviação Naval Brasileira* (Rio de Janeiro: Action Editora, 1995)

Gaspari, Elio, *A Ditadura Envergonhada. As Ilusões Armadas*, Vol. I (São Paulo: Cia das Letras, 2002)

Gaspari, Elio, *A Ditadura Escancarada. As Ilusões Armadas*, Vol. II (São Paulo: Cia das Letras, 2003)

Gaspari, Elio, *A Ditadura Derrotada. O Sacerdote e o Feiticeiro*, Vol. III (São Paulo: Cia das Letras, 2004)

Gaspari, Elio, *A Ditadura Encurralada. O Sacerdote e o Feiticeiro*, Vol. IV (São Paulo: Cia das Letras, 2002)

Gaspari, Elio, *A Ditadura Acabada*, Vol. V (São Paulo: Cia das Letras, 2016)

Hagedorn, Dan, *Texans and Harvards in Latin America* (West Sussex, UK: Air Britain Historians Ltd, 2009)

Hagedorn, Dan & Mario Overall, *Douglas DC-3/C-47 in Latin American Military Service* (Manchester: Crécy Publishing Ltd, 2021)

Higuchi, Hélio, Reginaldo Bacchi & Paulo Roberto Bastos Jr., *O Stuart No Brasil. M3/M3A1 e derivados*, 1ª Edição (São Paulo: Tecnodefesa Editorial Ltda, 2015)

Higuchi, Hélio & Paulo Roberto Bastos Jr., *M4 Sherman No Brasil*, Grandes Armas (São Paulo: C&R Editorial, 2008)

INCAER, *Historia Geral da Aeronáutica Brasileira*, Coleção Aeronáutica, Vol. 5 (Rio de Janeiro: Instituto Histórico-Cultural da Aeronáutica, 2014)

INCAER, *Historia Geral da Aeronáutica Brasileira*, Coleção Aeronáutica, Vol. 6 (Rio de Janeiro: Instituto Histórico-Cultural da Aeronáutica, 2022)

Klein, Herbert S. & Francisco Vidal Luna, *Brazil 1964–1985. The Military Regimes of Latin American in the Cold War* (London: Yale University Press, 2017)

Lavenére-Wanderley, Tenente-Brigadeiro R/R Nelson Freire, *História da Força Aérea Brasileira*, 2a. Edição (Rio de Janeiro: INCAER, 1975)

Lorch, Carlos, *Fuzileiros Navais, Brazil's Amphibious Warriors* (Rio de Janeiro: Action Editora, 1999)

Mattos de Abreu, Guilherme; Barbosa Junior, Ilques; de Senna Bittencourt, Armando; Carmo Cesar, William; Gomes dos Santos Filho, Pedro; Eduardo Alves de Almeida, Francisco; de Sousa Moreira, William; Laura Costa Nogueira da Gama, Edina; Oliveira Castro, Alceu; Jungstedt; Paulo da Cunha Castro, Pierre; André Lopes da Silva, Carlos; dos Santos Guimarães, Ricardo; José Gomes Loureiro, Marcello; Homero Fonseca de Castro, Adler; & de Freitas e Gonzaga da Silva, Jéssica, *Marinha do Brasil: Uma Síntese Histórica* (Rio de Janeiro: Serviço de Documentação da Marinha, 2022)

Monteiro, Adalberto *et al.*, *Guerrilha do Araguaia* (São Paulo: Anita Garibaldi Editora, 2005)

Morais, Taís & Eumano Silva, *Operação Araguaia. Os Arquivos Secretos da Guerrilha* (São Paulo: Geração Editorial, 2011)

Nascimento, Durbens, *A Guerrilha do Araguaia 1967–1975. Paulistas e Militares na Amazonía* (Belém, Pará: NAEA Editora, 2021)

Nascimento, José & Licio Maciel, *Orvil Tentativas De Tomada Do Poder* (Salto, SP: Editora Schoba, 2009)

Pereira Netto, Francisco C., *Aviação Militar Brasileira 1916–1984* (Rio de Janeiro: Revista Aeronáutica Editora, 1984)

Portela, Fernando, *Guerras e Guerrilhas no Brasil* (São Paulo: Global Editora, 1979)

Skidmore, Thomas E., *The Politics of Military Rule in Brazil, 1964–1985* (New York: Oxford University Press, 1988)

Studart, Hugo, *A lei da selva: estratégias, imaginário e discurso dos militares sobre a guerrilha do Araguaia* (São Paulo: Geração Editorial, 2006)

Ustra, Carlos Alberto Brilhante, *A Verdade Sufocada* (Brasília: Editora Ser, 2006)

Articles

De Almeida Teles, Janaina, 'Secrets and Myths about the Araguaia Guerrilla War' (1972–1974), *Historia Unisinos*, Vol. 18, No. 3 (Universidade do Vale do Rio dos Sinos, São Leopoldo, September-December 2014)

De Souza Pinheiro, Cel. EB Álvaro, 'Guerrilla in the Brazilian Amazon', *FMSO Publications* (Foreign Military Studies Office, Fort Leavenworth, KS, July 1995)

Maklouf Carvalho, Cel. FAB Luiz, 'A FAB usou Napalm no Araguaia', *Air & Space Power Journal* (1998)

Munhoz Svartman, Eduardo, 'Brazil–United States Relations during the Cold War: Political Dynamic and Arms Transfers', *Brazilian Political Science Review (BPSR)*, Vol. 5, No.2 (2011, Associação Brasileira de Ciencia Política, São Paulo)

Navarro V, Lic. Agustín, 'Los Grupos Revolucionarios del Brasil', *Temas Contemporáneos*, Año XVI, No. 198 (México: Instituto de Investigaciones Sociales y Económicas A.C., 1971)

Pinheiro, Coronel Álvaro de Souza, *Guerrilha na Amazônia: Uma Experiência no Passado, Presente e o Futuro* (Washington, DC: Air Power Journal, edição trimestral de abril/maio/junho, 1995)

Teló, Fabricio, 'Campesinos, emociones y tentativas de resistencia armada a la dictadura empresarial-militar de Brasil', *Polis Revista Latinoamericana*, No. 53, Centro de Investigación Sociedad y Políticas Públicas (CISPO) (31 May 2019, Universidad Federal Rural de Rio de Janeiro)

Conferences

Morales, Vanessa, 'Las Guerrillas de Araguaia. La última guerrilla comunista'. Conference during the XIII Jornadas de Sociología, Facultad de Ciencias Sociales, Universidad de Buenos Aires, Buenos Aires, 2019

Nercesian, Inés, 'Nueva Izquierda en Brasil en los años 60'. Conference during the VI Jornadas de Sociología, Facultad de Ciencias Sociales, Universidad de Buenos Aires, Buenos Aires, 2004

University Papers

Almeida, Thamyris F.T., *Araguaia: Maoist Uprising and Military Counterinsurgency in the Brazilian Amazon, 1967–1975* (Master's Degree thesis, University of Massachusetts Amherst, July 2015)

Oliveira, Juliano, *Força Aérea Brasileira: doctrina e estrutura da geopolítica do Prata a Amazónia, 1964–2003)* (Master's Degree thesis, Universidade Estadual Paulista/UNESP, Franca, SP, 2005)

Pessoa Campos Filho, Romualdo, *A Esquerda em Armas: História da Guerrilha do Araguaia (1972–1975)*, Dissertação apresentada no curso de pós-graduação do Instituto de Ciências Humanas e Letras da Universidade Federal de Goiás para o mestrado em História das Sociedades Agrárias em fevereiro de 1995

Web Pages

Araguaia Guerrilla, at https://www.todamateria.com.br/guerrilha-do-araguaia/

Brazilian Army reorganization, at https://pt.wikipedia.org/wiki/Reorganizao_do_Exercito_Brasileiro_na_ditadura_militar

Brazilian tanks and armored vehicles, at https://tanks-encyclopedia.com/coldwar/brazilian-tanks/

Brazilian Naval Aviation, at
https://asassobreosmares.rudnei.cunha.nom.br/category/historia/

https://www.jornalopcao.com.br/colunas-e-blogs/imprensa/ordem-pra-matar-na-guerrilha-do-araguaia-era-do-presidente-emilio-medici-diz-o-coronel-pedro-cabral-426274/

'Guerrilha na Amazonía: Uma experiencia no pasado, o presente e o fututo', article published by Cel. Álvaro de Souza Pinheiro do Exército Brasileiro in November 2005 at https://www.defesanet.com.br/geopolitica/noticia/5193/toa-guerrilha-na-amazonia-a-experiencia-dos-anos-70-parte-2/

Brazilian Navy ships, at
https://pt.wikipedia.org/wiki/Lista_de_navios_descomissionados_da_Marinha_do_Brasil

Brazilian police forces, at
https://pt.wikipedia.org/wiki/Forças_policiais_do_Brasil

ABOUT THE AUTHOR

Antonio Luis Sapienza Fracchia was born in Asunción, Paraguay, on 14 May 1960. He graduated from the Catholic University of Asunción, where he got a B.A. in Clinical Psychology. He also took specialised English courses at Tulane University in New Orleans, Louisiana, and teaching methodology courses at San Diego State University in California. He is now retired but worked for nearly 40 years as an English teacher and one of the academic coordinators at the *Centro Cultural Paraguayo-Americano* (CCPA), a binational institute in Asunción. Married with two children, he resides in the capital. He is an aviation historian who has written more than 500 articles in specialised magazines and web pages on the history of Paraguayan aviation and has given numerous lectures in schools, universities, institutes and military and civil institutions in Paraguay and abroad. Since 2004, he has been an aviation history professor in the Paraguayan Air Force (FAP). In August 2023, he was appointed Corresponding Academician of the Paraguayan Academy of History. He has published 27 books since 1996, this being his 14th with Helion. He has received a total of seven decorations for his academic merits: two from Argentina, one from Brazil and four from his own country, Paraguay (two from the Air Force, one from the Naval Aviation and one from the Civil Aviation Authority DINAC).